GW01071922

Principles of
Social Welfare

Principles of Social Welfare

An introduction to thinking about the Welfare State

PAUL SPICKER

Routledge

London & New York

First published in 1988 by
Routledge
11 New Fetter Lane, London EC4P 4EE
29 West 35th Street, New York NY 10001

© 1988 Paul Spicker

Typeset by Scarborough Typesetting Services
Printed in Great Britain by
Richard Clay Ltd, Bungay, Suffolk

British Library Cataloguing in Publication Data
Spicker, Paul
    Principles of social welfare: an
    introduction to thinking about the welfare
    state.
    1. Welfare state
    I. Title
    361.6'5

Library of Congress Cataloging in Publication Data
Spicker, Paul.
    Principles of social welfare: an
    introduction to thinking about the
    welfare state/Paul Spicker.
        p.   cm.
    Bibliography: p.
    Includes index.
    1. Social policy.   2. Welfare state.
    3. Public welfare.
    I. Title.
    HN16.S67   1988
    361.6'1—dc 19

ISBN 0-415-00630-9
ISBN 0-415-00631-7 Pbk

Contents

PART 1

Individual and social welfare

I

Welfare

Summary: Welfare provision serves mainly the physical and material interests of recipients. Interests are linked both with people's needs, which are socially defined, and with what people want. If people can be mistaken about where their interests lie, their welfare will not be served by considering their wants alone.

Social welfare is not simply the sum of individual welfares, and one concept cannot be derived from the other. Some interests may be held in common. Equally, however, there may be conflicts between interests, and some may bear costs for the benefit of others.

In its broadest sense, the idea of 'welfare' refers to 'well-being', or what is 'good' for people. Understood more narrowly, it can be taken to refer to the provision of social services – principally health care, housing, social security, education, and social work. The connection between the two uses rests in the role of social services as 'the provision of welfare'. Part of the purpose of social services is, ideally, altruistic – 'doing good' to people. There are curative approaches: people who have something wrong with them receive 'treatment' to put it right. Social services can be developmental: a society in which individuals are valued should have the facilities to help them realize their potential. And social services may protect people; the 'safety net' which the services provide helps to remove the uncertainty associated with need, a protection against for example the problems of old age, disability, or poverty.

However, the provision of welfare is not necessarily for the benefit of the recipients alone. Townsend suggests that 'social services are those means developed and institutionalised by society to promote ends which are wholly or primarily social' (Townsend 1976: 28). In many ways, measures which benefit the individual person are important for society: societies are, after all, made up of people. But there are also aims which can be seen as more for the benefit of the whole society than for any person within it. The social services can, for example, reinforce economic policy. They can be seen as a way to achieve equality or social justice. They may be an instrument of social change. They can also, conversely, be a means of maintaining social order. The provision of welfare is contentious. There are many different and conflicting views of what is good for the individual or society. This book is an examination of the principles which guide such judgements. Its aim is to explain the values which are being applied, to examine the grounds on which disagreements of principle arise, and to relate principles to practical issues of welfare provision.

INDIVIDUAL WELFARE

We refer to what is 'good' for people as being in their *interests* – interests being those things which lead to well-being. Feinberg uses the term 'welfare interests' to refer to the interests that he considers fundamental. They include physical health and vigour; physical integrity and functioning; the absence of pain or disfigurement; a minimum degree of intellectual activity; emotional stability; the absence of groundless anxieties and resentments; engagement in a normal social life; a minimum amount of wealth, income, and financial security; a tolerable social and physical environment; and some freedom from interference by others (Feinberg 1980: 32). These interests are 'basic', in his view, because without them a person cannot be a person. In other words, welfare interests are *needs* – items that are essential.

Maslow writes, as a psychologist, about a 'hierarchy' of needs, a series of conditions which must be met for each person.

There are at least five sets of goals which we may call basic needs. These are briefly physiological, safety, love, esteem and self-actualisation. . . . These basic goals are related to one another, being arranged in a hierarchy of prepotency. This means that the most prepotent goal will monopolise consciousness. . . . The less prepotent needs are minimised, even forgotten or denied. But when a need is fairly well satisfied, the next prepotent (higher) need emerges.

(Maslow 1943: 395)

In other words, physiological needs are more important than safety, safety than the need for love, and so on. There are three main problems with this concept. In the first place, Maslow's order of priority is debatable – is love really subordinate to safety? Second, it is not clear that basic needs can be ordered in a 'hierarchy' at all. In some cases, the value of measures to look after a person's physiological needs is clearly reduced if other needs are not met; many people would prefer to be malnourished and free rather than to be well-fed in prison. This implies that people are affected, no so much by a hierarchy, as by a whole set of interdependent needs. Third, it is difficult to apply the approach directly to the provision of welfare. Education is almost certainly of less importance than a person's emotional needs, but education is largely organized as a social service, and provision for emotional needs is not. If there is a pressing need for state-run computer dating, the case has not been made out. On the face of it, the concept of 'welfare' seems to take in every aspect of a person's life – physical, emotional, material, and spiritual. Robson, writing about the 'welfare state', emphasizes that 'welfare is of unlimited scope' (Robson 1976: 174). But in practice, the concept is rather more limited than a general concern with 'well-being' would suggest. In the context of social policy, the idea of 'welfare' refers primarily to physical and material well-being – not because the areas of emotional and spiritual life are irrelevant but because it is normally considered to be beyond the scope of the social services to provide for them.

The sorts of areas in which 'needs' are commonly taken to occur include, Harvey suggests, food, housing, medical care, education, social and environmental service, consumer goods, recreational opportunities, neighbourhood amenities, and transport facilities (Harvey 1973: 102). The exclusion of employment opportunities from this list is, as Jones and his colleagues note, an illustration of the way in which ideas of need change over time (Jones, Brown and Bradshaw 1978: 28). It is fairly easy to add other needs to the list: they might include physical care (like help in bathing or dressing), clothing, fuel, or simply the money to buy things. But the list is not infinite; to a large extent, it is limited to those areas in which some sort of social provision might be made. The statement that people are in 'need', that they *must* have something, effectively constitutes a claim against other people to make some sort of response.

Within each category of need there are degrees of classification –
'greater' or 'lesser' needs – depending on how strong the claim is and
how 'essential' the need appears to be. An example of this is *poverty*,
the lack of material resources. People are not simply said to be 'poor'
or 'not poor'; they may be destitute (almost totally without resources),
poor, deprived, or disadvantaged. Within these categories there are
further gradations – like 'very poor', 'poor', 'fairly' poor. These are
not precise terms with a universally agreed meaning, and they may
overlap with the other categories; there is no clear distinction, for
example, between 'fairly poor' and 'deprived'. In the case of other
'needs', there are gradations made between those things which are
needed more and those which are needed less. This may mean either
that both things are necessary, but one is more important than the
other; or that a condition has only been partially satisfied. People in
general need food to live, and to be healthy; the food might be
enough to preserve life but not health. A person without any food at
all is more 'in need' than someone who does not have food which is
adequately nutritious, but it makes perfectly good sense to talk about
both people as being 'in need' – which means that both people have a
claim, even if one claim is stronger than the other.

Bradshaw distinguishes two different types of need, *normative* and
comparative, which represent claims of different types (Bradshaw
1972). Normative need is established by experts, as a fixed level;
comparative need is based on a comparison with others. Poverty
again provides a clear example. It is usually separated into two main
concepts, absolute and relative. *Absolute poverty* describes a minimum
standard needed to live, or 'subsistence'. Charles Booth, in his studies
of Victorian England, identified the main basic needs as food,
clothing, fuel and shelter, and treated people as 'poor' when they
lacked enough money to satisfy these needs. Seebohm Rowntree's
work later distinguished *primary poverty*, where people have less than
is necessary for subsistence, from *secondary poverty*, where they fall
below the subsistence level because of the way in which they spend
their money. (His purpose in doing this was not to show how badly
the poor managed their money; he was trying to counter the
argument that people were poor because of mismanagement. His
survey showed that even if people managed their budget perfectly,
allowed themselves no luxuries and walked everywhere, many

people would still be in primary poverty. See Veit Wilson 1983.) Both of these studies depend on the view that poverty can be clearly and explicitly defined in terms of minimum needs.

Relative poverty is based on a comparison of poor people with others in society. A person who would be considered 'poor' in Britain might be 'well off' in the terms of the Third World. Different standards are being applied, based on comparisons within societies rather than between them. This definition, however, compounds two different ideas. The first is that people are poor by comparison with others – for example, because their income is in the lowest 10 per cent of the population, or because they fall significantly below the average income. The second idea is drawn from the Marxist tradition. Marx argued that although some human needs are basic to everyone, the pattern and interpretation of those needs is socially defined (Marx 1844: 87–96). This may still mean that a level can be fixed in the context of a particular society, based on accepted standards rather than on comparisons between groups. 'Homelessness', for example, is a socially determined issue. In many countries, people without a home of their own build squatter shacks; it is a normal pattern of development in some Third World countries (see Turner 1969). In Britain, people are not allowed to build a home where or how they can, and the problem of homelessness is an obvious result. (This is not to say that squatter settlements are a better way of dealing with the lack of shelter; they present a different kind of problem.) Poverty, in the same way, is defined by the conditions prevalent in a particular society. In the Soviet Union the official standard of poverty is based in a 'subsistence' standard. This is justified by the argument that the amount needed for subsistence is determined by the conditions in that country (McAuley 1977). Peter Townsend describes poverty as 'the absence or inadequacy of those diets, amenities, standards, services and activities which are common or customary in society. People are deprived of the conditions of life which customarily define membership of society' (Townsend 1979: 915). This is a complex idea: it combines the Marxist view with a comparative standard, based on objective circumstances, and the idea of 'relative deprivation', which is based in attitudes. It has been influential in the study of social policy but it is not uncontentious. It is robustly rejected by Joseph (a former Conservative Secretary of State responsible for Health and Social Security) and Sumption: 'A family is poor if it cannot afford to eat. It is not poor if it cannot afford endless smokes and it does not become poor by the mere fact that other people can afford them' (Joseph and Sumption 1979: 27). There are two main problems with Townsend's definition. In the first place, virtually everyone in a society may be poor, in the sense of lacking material resources, but they could not be considered poor if standards are defined in terms of what is 'common' or 'customary'. Marshall writes about 'relative poverty' that 'If it means that poverty is relative to the standard of civilisation of the country concerned, it is beyond dispute. If it means that I may not say that A is poor, but only that he is poorer than B, I cannot accept it' (Marshall 1981: 116-17). The other main objection to his approach is that it extends the idea of 'poverty' to cover almost all forms of disadvantage, which is not the way that 'poverty' is generally seen. Poverty refers to the most serious deprivation: Marshall argues that 'the common factor in the state of the poor is the urgency of their need' (*ibid.*: 117). Townsend's extension of the term is an attempt to emphasize the claims of all those who are deprived; in doing so, he may be weakening the claim of those whose deprivation is worst.

NEEDS AND WANTS

Bradshaw distinguishes two other categories of need: *felt need* and *expressed need* (Bradshaw 1972). The terms are fairly self-explanatory; felt need is what people feel they must have, and expressed need is a strongly expressed want. The distinction between them is that a person can feel a need without telling other people about it – people are sometimes reluctant to claim services because of fear, apprehension, or stigma – and it is possible to express a need without feeling it. Unlike normative and comparative concepts of need, these categories are formed by the people in need themselves.

Interests can be categorized in a similar way: they can be decided by the person who has them, or by other who apply different standards to the circumstances of the individual. Little, in a critique of welfare economics, identifies welfare with 'happiness' (Little 1957, Ch. 5). 'Happiness' is a mental state or point of view. It is a value-laden term because it suggests that individual feelings are important; one might argue that only an individual can really tell if he or she is happy, and it seems to follow that individuals are likely to be the best judge of their own welfare. 'Welfare' seems, on this basis, to be closely linked to individual choices and desires. Dahl, a political scientist firmly committed to the American model of democracy, argues that interests can only be identified by the people who have them, which tends to identify interests directly with wants (Dahl 1961). However, what people want or choose is not always something that is good for them. People can make the wrong choices; they may be better off if they are steered in another direction. Barry links interests with those things which lead to the satisfaction of wants (Barry 1965). It is not necessarily in a child's interests to stay off school, even if the child wants to play instead, because ultimately schooling increases one's opportunities for wants to be satisfied.

There is certainly a link between the satisfaction of wants and a person's welfare. But if people can be mistaken about where their interests lie, their welfare will not be served by considering their wants alone. Jordan suggests that a person's interests are best defined by reference to that person's 'life-plan' (Jordan 1987b: 18–19), which covers, not only what people currently want, but what they are likely to want in the future. Interests may, then, overlap with expressed desires, but they might not; the two concepts are distinct. Goodin argues that opinion is shaped by experience, and that values and perceptions of interests change constantly (Goodin 1982, Ch. 3). If popular opinion had been the test, it is doubtful whether there would be any social security system in the United States, and if it is taken as the test in the future, there may never be a National Health Service there. He describes the emphasis on what people want as 'myopic' (*ibid.*: p.42).

Giddens points to interests as implying the satisfaction of 'unconscious' wants: 'Since men are not necessarily aware of their motives for acting in a particular way, they are not necessarily aware of what in any given situation their given interests are either' (Giddens 1976: 86). This moves towards the view that interests are not directly observable, but have to be analysed. Everyone really 'wants' what is best for them. Unconscious wants – the wants they may not realize they have – are the wants they should have if they knew the likely consequences. The danger in this approach is fairly clear; it effectively justifies the imposition of one assessment of interests over another. It could be argued that what people happen to want is less important than what is in their interests; but in pretending that people want things without realizing it, the formula tries to have it both ways, accepting that what people want is important while rejecting what they say. Marx goes a step further, by saying that capitalist society creates 'false' needs which mislead people as to where their true interests lie (Heller 1976). This is tantamount to saying that what people think they want is irrelevant.

Barry refers to principles which respect what people express as in their interests as *want-regarding* (Barry 1965: 187–8). Other principles, taking other values into account, are *ideal-regarding* – a classification which includes Giddens's 'unconscious' interests. Welfare, Barry argues, takes into account both what people want and what is good for them. It is necessarily, then, a mixture of want-regarding and ideal-regarding principles. This is a reasonable enough position, but it does not help us come to any firm conclusion about exactly what 'welfare' might be in a particular case. What it does, instead, is to mark out an area of uncertainty – an area in which one cannot say with absolute confidence that a measure does make someone 'better off'.

SOCIAL WELFARE

The discussion of 'need' and 'welfare' so far has been based on people as 'individuals'. One view of 'society' is that it consists simply of many individuals; 'social welfare', therefore, is nothing but the sum of individual welfares. Oakeshott, a conservative political philosopher, condemns the idea of society as an abstraction; it implies, he argues, some association between people without specifying what the association is (Oakeshott 1975: 340). Jeremy Bentham, who historically must be considered one of the most important writers on welfare issues, argued that 'The community is a fictitious body, composed of the individual persons who are considered as constituting as it were its members. The interest of the community is, then, what? – the sum of the interests of the several members who compose it' (Bentham

1789: 35). This view is basic to traditional welfare economics. Sugden
points to three principal value judgements (Sugden 1980: 166).

(1) Each person is on the face of it the best judge of his or her own
    welfare.
(2) Social welfare depends on the welfare of individuals; there is no
    such thing as the welfare of a society, through, for example, its
    culture or collective existence, which is not directly attributable
    to the welfare of individuals.
(3) If one person's welfare increases, and no-one else's decreases,
    there has been an increase in social welfare. (This last point is
    contentious, because it could mean that increased inequality is
    acceptable if it does not make others worse off. The issues are
    discussed further in Chapters 8 to 10 below.)

There are, however, few measures of social welfare provision which
leave absolutely no-one worse off – if only because someone,
somewhere has to pay for them. The main exceptions are measures
which increase both *efficiency* and *effectiveness*. Efficiency depends on
the relationship between aims and costs; the most efficient measure is
the one that yields the best result at least cost, but the constraint of ?
cost means that something less than the maximum goal may be
achieved. Effectiveness depends on maximizing the achievement of
goals. Efficiency and effectiveness are sometimes elevated to the
status of principles, because they are the means to increase welfare;
in fact they are secondary to other principles because their impor- ?
tance derives from the aims they are serving.

    In social planning, cost–benefit analysis (CBA) has become an
important tool. CBA tries to measure all the costs of a policy or ɛvaᴌ⟍ɑтɩₒⱴ₴
programme against all the benefits which come out of it. The great
advantage of CBA, and the reason for its increasing use, is that it
helps at least to make explicit the likely consequences of certain
policy decisions. An example is the case of child-proofed drug
containers, estimated in the early 1970s to cost half a million pounds
each year. The government at first thought the cost was too high, but
were persuaded to meet it when it was argued they would save some
16,000 admissions to hospital and perhaps twenty deaths each year.
This is an example of a more efficient way to avoid problems which
are detrimental to welfare – though the fact the calculation had to be

Table 1.1 *The greatest happiness of the greatest number*

	Programme A	Programme B	Programme C
Tom	5	4	12
Dick	5	4	0
Harry	1	4	3
Total welfare	11	12	15

Source: Adapted from Bowie and Simon 1977: 39.

made raises questions about the apparent value placed on a child's life.

Another illustration of CBA in practice is the decision to place crash barriers on motorways. The effect of these barriers is to reduce the number of fatal accidents, because cars are less likely to collide with traffic coming in the opposite direction, but to increase the number of accidents which are not fatal. In effect, the risks – and the costs borne – are being redistributed on the basis of the relative value placed on different kinds of accident. (These, and other examples, can be found in Mooney, Russell, and Weir 1980, Ch. 7.)

There are a number of assumptions underlying CBA. The first is that individual welfare can be measured in terms which can be added together or taken away from each other to yield an end result. Second, it can be calculated in terms of money, which means that monetary values are taken to reflect social values. Third, social welfare is increased if the total welfare of the people in society is increased – despite the fact that some people will be worse off.

The rationale for this position stems from utilitarianism, a philosophical doctrine which holds that the promotion of welfare, or 'utility', is the basis of moral decisions. The utility of a whole society consists of the sum of the utilities of its members. Bentham argued that social welfare should be seen as 'the greatest happiness of the greatest number'. This formula is superficially appealing, but it is not without its problems. Consider the effect of three programmes on the distribution of resources – or, for the sake of argument, 'units of happiness' – between three people, Tom, Dick, and Harry (Table 1.1). Programme C produces the highest total – the greatest 'social welfare' if welfare is taken to be the sum of individual welfares.

Table 1.2 *The Condorcet effect*

	Programme A	Programme B	Programme C
Tom	2nd	3rd	1st
Dick	1st	2nd	3rd
Harry	3rd	1st	2nd

Programme A leads to greater happiness for a majority of people than Programme B. B makes more people happy than A or C, and it leads to less suffering – another possible criterion – but less total happiness than C, and it leaves a majority worse off than A. The question of which constitutes the 'greatest happiness of the greatest number' is unclear. The problem is that the interests of the members of a community may conflict. It becomes, as a result, difficult to claim that any resolution clearly represents the interest of a community rather than of a faction which is part of it.

It is possible to show formally that a view of social welfare as a majority preference cannot validly be derived from information about individual preferences. The proof is named after the Marquis de Condorcet, who first demonstrated it. It is not easy to follow at first, but it is worth the effort. Two main premises are required, but they are not at all difficult to accept.

(1) Rational preferences are *non-reflexive*. This means that if X is preferred to Y, then Y cannot at the same time be preferred to X.

(2) Rational preferences are *transitive*: if X is preferred to Y, and Y to Z, then X is preferred to Z.

Suppose that Tom, Dick, and Harry have been asked to choose between the three programmes mentioned before. The choices they make are, unsurprising (Table 1.2). Now, Tom, Dick, and Harry have all made rational choices, for their own reasons – in the example here, because they have chosen programmes according to their immediate personal interests. However, the combined effect of these choices is inconsistent.

The majority (Tom and Dick) prefer A to B.

The majority (Dick and Harry) prefer B to C.

Now, if A is preferred to B, and B to C, then A should be preferred to C. But the majority (Tom and Harry) prefer C to A. What has happened is that *rational individual choices have led to an irrational majority preference*. It follows from this that we cannot validly make assumptions about the preferences of the majority from the preferences of individuals – not because the preferences will fall out this way, but because they might, and it is impossible to be sure that the right questions have been asked in the right order. The choices of a society have to be made in some other way – a problem which, Arrow argues, implies an imposed solution (Arrow 1967).

The Condorcet effect is a model, not of social welfare as such, but of social choice. 'Preferences', as noted before, are not directly equivalent to interests; what people choose is not necessarily what is good for them. But choice and welfare are still related to each other, and in the case of Tom, Dick, and Harry, any attempt to select a solution on the basis of the welfare of the majority meets with all the same objections. It is not valid, then, to determine the welfare of the majority on the basis of the welfare of individuals. It would be easy to exaggerate the importance of this argument. It is a strictly formal proof, and there is no obvious reason why policies and programmes should have to be decided with any degree of logical consistency. Its main value is to stress that 'society' cannot be seen simply as an aggregation of individuals, and that it is arguable whether social welfare can actually be seen as an aggregate interest – the sum of individual welfares – at all.

THE COMMON GOOD

The 'individuals' of moral and political philosophy are not like real people. Real people live in families, groups, and communities; they learn values and ideas from each other. Opinions, views, and preferences may differ, but they are not formed in a vacuum. There may be a general consensus about certain values. There may be shared interests. White argues, from a conservative perspective, that 'society is not a collection of "universalised individuals", nor the sum of individuals statistically aggregated, but the product of a system of real relationships between individuals, classes, groups and interests' (White, in Buck 1975: 176). When we consider the idea of 'social welfare' in practice, we tend to refer not to individual preferences but to groups of people who have interests in common. Old people

have diverse problems, but by virtue of their age they share
concerns about, for example, policies for retirement, pensions,
and the maintenance of health. Children require education, material stability, and emotional support. Everyone is first a child,
and most of us expect to become old; these concerns are likely to
affect all of us in some way. But pensions, schooling, and medical
care are not universal truths of human nature. The ways in which
the problems are defined, and policies are formed to deal with
them, depend on the society in which they occur. People may
differ in their choices, or in their views as to how these issues are
best dealt with, but the interests apply to these groups as a whole,
and through them to every member of a society. There is a *common
good*, a concept of social welfare distinct from the welfare of
individuals.

The idea of the 'common good' is rich in ambiguity. It may be
taken to mean, at times, that each person has an interest which
others also have – we all need to eat, to have shelter, and so forth –
and the common good is a concept which recognizes the interests
of each person. Jordan refers to the 'reciprocity' which binds
together the members of a society – a principle which means, in
this context, that everyone recognizes the claims of others in order
to have their own interests respected (Jordan 1987a). To take a
simple example, since no-one wants to be murdered in bed, there
is a reciprocal advantage in everyone agreeing that the act should
be forbidden. This principle, taken to its logical conclusion, is the
basis of the concept of national insurance. Insurance involves the
pooling of resources to protect each person against risk. If everyone is at risk of poverty, sickness, or death, a system which
provides mutual protection in these contingencies is taken to be in
everyone's interest. Jordan proposes a model of social welfare
which is clearly opposed to individualist values.

(1) Each individual's welfare depends on needs which he or she
    is not capable of meeting by his or her efforts alone.
(2) Social welfare depends on co-operation and social solidarity.
(3) Social welfare is therefore something more than, and
    different from the welfare of individuals.

(Jordan 1987b: 42)

However, if Jordan is right to accept in the first place that the interests of each person can be distinguished from other people's, it can be argued that his idea of a common good is nothing more than the sum of the welfare of individuals, seen from a different perspective. People may have interests not only as individuals but also as members of a community. Jordan suggests that in cases where there is a common threat, people 'co-operate to reduce the risks of all' (Jordan 1987a). The outstanding example is national defence in wartime, when each individual is considered to be affected by the threat to the whole. It may be in these cases that some individuals have personal positions which conflict with the good of others – for example, a trader who loses business with the enemy power – in which case it is possible to say that their interests as individuals conflict with their interests as a member of a group. National insurance can be represented in a similar way. It is often justified, in Europe, on the basis of 'social solidarity'. On the face of it, this is surprising; contributions and benefits are related clearly to each person as an individual. But the cost of paying for national insurance is not necessarily in keeping with the risk which each person faces as an individual. If those individuals whose risks were lower did not participate in the system of insurance, the effect would be to increase the costs to those whose risks were greater, and the effect for the community as a whole would be to reduce its power to protect its members. This argument extends beyond positions where people are considered to be at risk, to others where there is some positive benefit to be gained for everyone. The justification for building parks or roads is that they are 'social goods', with a value to each person as a member of the community which outweighs the costs to any one individual. The 'common good' may, then, refer not only to interests which other people also have, but to interests which are shared by everyone in a community to some degree.

The strongest concept of the 'common good' is based in the good of society as a whole. Titmuss writes that 'All collectively provided services are deliberately designed to meet certain socially recognised needs; they are manifestations . . . of society's will to survive as an organic whole' (Titmuss 1955a: 39). The idea that society has a 'will', or that it can be seen as an 'organic' unit like a plant, is very arguable.

But it is possible to conceive of society as a unit with interests that are potentially distinct from the interests of its individual members. A society without children could not survive into the future; one of the justifications for child allowances is that they represent social support for people to have children. A society without workers would not be able to function: a 'work ethic', emphasizing the value of work and the contribution that people make to society, is not only a feature of the capitalist societies of the west; it is vigorously enforced in communist states with a collectivist ethos (see Beerman 1960). Social services protect and stabilize the industrial process. Social security acts as an economic regulator; education benefits industry by training workers, and later by looking after their children during the day; the health service keeps them fit for work. These are what Titmuss calls the *handmaiden* functions – welfare as the handmaiden of the process of production (Titmuss 1974). In order to continue to exist, a society has to have some means of maintaining order, of surviving change, and of reproducing itself in the future. The promotion of welfare can be seen as essential to these aims.

WELFARE IN SOCIETY

When 'social welfare' is discussed, we do not necessarily begin by talking about 'individuals'; we are just as likely to talk about 'society', and to think of individuals as members of it. Little argues: 'Most people who consider the welfare of society do not, I am sure, think of it as a logical construction from the welfares of individuals. They think rather in terms of social or economic groups, or in terms of average or representative men' (Little 1957: 49). The danger of this approach, he warns, is that it is possible to lose sight of real people (many of whom are not 'men' at all).

> The tastes of an average man do not change at all rapidly. He does not experiment very much. His life is not subject to any shocks or crises . . . . His position on the social scale will not alter very much. The welfare of his friends and relatives is unlikely to alter greatly. Much more important, he never dies.
>
> (*ibid.*: 49)

The criticism is a justifiable one. When we say that a measure will benefit 'old people' in general, we know that some of them will be dead before any improvement takes place. This would not be a reason for not undertaking the programme, because it will still help the representative person. However, there is also the risk that concentration on the 'average' member of society might lead to sacrifices on the part of specific individuals or minority interests who are unrepresentative. An illustration of this in practice has been the use of slum clearance in urban areas. Many of the houses demolished were irredeemable; houses, like everything else, wear out. The removal of the worst slums, and rehousing into better physical conditions, certainly benefited many individuals – though the social costs of clearance were great, and the policy was not always unequivocally beneficial. Clearance commonly took place at the expense of certain individuals who were content with their house and did not want to move. As a former housing officer myself, I had to explain to people why their houses could not be excluded from the programme – for example, because it was not really feasible to knock down all the houses in a terrace except for one in the middle; because the environment they wanted to stay in was being destroyed; because the land their house was on was going to be used for a new school or road and it was impossible to build it round them. The interests of the group or community, and of the representative member of society, were served by clearance; but those interests were directly opposed to the people who wanted to stay. Welfare, in these cases, totters perilously close to becoming the 'greatest good of the greatest number'.

Ideally, it may be possible to harmonize the interests of each person with those of the wider community – an aim referred to as 'social integration'. 'By and large', Boulding writes, 'it is an objective of social policy to build the identity of a person around some community with which he is associated' (Boulding 1973: 192). This implies that the individual, acting as a member of the community, will identify his or her welfare with that of the group. A UN report suggests that a basic aim of social services is to help

towards a mutual adjustment of individuals and their social environment. This objective is achieved through the use of techniques and methods which are designed to help individuals,

WELFARE 19

groups and communities to solve their problems of adjustment to a
changing pattern of society.

(quoted in Greve 1975: 184–5)

The purpose is not, as Greve points out, intended only to change
people, but to make society adjust to them (Greve 1975: 185). But
there are two sides to the coin. The 'treatment' of individuals may be
a way of compelling them to fit in with society – the treatment of
mental illness to prevent danger to others is an illustration; helping
people to solve problems may become, in practice, passive dependency; and the mutual adjustment of society and the individual may
degenerate into social control. Social services can reinforce a social
order by making social structures publicly acceptable. They can press
people to conform, imposing a morality on their recipients. They can
foster exploitation. In some cases, they may become directly re-
pressive.

The idea of 'social welfare' appears, in form, to refer to the
'common good', improvements that benefit almost everyone in
society, a ground for consensus. In practice there may be conflicts of
interest. There are likely to be losers as well as gainers, *dis*welfare as
well as welfare. The value bases on which these conflicts are judged
form a major part of the discussion of this book.

II

Social norms

Summary: *Moral principles are socially defined. Moral norms are generally accepted rules which are considered particularly important and which assume some personal responsibility for actions.*

Social services do not always enforce moral norms directly, but they tend to reinforce existing rules. Moral rules lead to the rejection of some people as deviant, and social services may exacerbate this by labelling people or by treating people as responsible for their condition.

Decisions about welfare are made within a framework of values. These values are not formed by individuals in isolation. The process is one which Berger and Luckmann describe as 'inter-subjective', depending on shared perceptions and views which people learn from each other (Berger and Luckmann 1967). Values are expressed as *social norms*. A norm is a generalized expectation about what people are or what they do – 'generalized' in the sense of referring to people in general rather than to specific individuals. It is 'social' when it is shared by a significant number of people in society.

Moral values are a category of social norms. There are of course many different kinds of expectations in society that are not moral. For example, we usually expect people to have two legs, and when they do not we tend to be surprised, to stare, perhaps to be embarrassed – even though it is not *that* extraordinary for people to have only one; the expectation is not a moral one. Needs are defined by expectations, which may or may not be moral. And the expectations associated with roles and status, important as they are, are also not usually seen as moral norms – though in some societies the preservation of status differentials is treated as a moral issue. Moral norms involve three main elements which distinguish them from other kinds of norm. First, moral norms involve judgements about behaviour. They usually assume that an individual is responsible for his or her actions, although there are exceptions to this: people who are mentally ill are sometimes treated as both evil and irresponsible. Another significant exception is the stigmatization of illegitimate children. This stems from a period when the family, not the individual, was seen as the primary social unit; it is difficult to see any basis for the moral rejection of illegitimacy from the viewpoint of individualism, in the same way as it is now difficult for many to accept the curse put upon families in the Bible even unto the third generation. In general, though, morality assumes individual autonomy. Second, moral norms are, for the most part, treated as serious and important. This is sometimes because of religious belief, sometimes because they affect others. Rules which do not seem quite so important – like whether a person says 'thank you' for a gift – are treated as matters of manners or etiquette. Third, moral norms are rules. People are not simply encouraged or expected to follow them but are required to obey. This most often means that there is a *sanction* or means of enforcing the rule – though so many moral rules are internalized, accepted without external enforcement, that the sanction may not be obvious.

Norms develop over time. Edmund Burke makes the case that they are adopted because they work; because they prove beneficial, they are 'written in' to social codes. He calls this process 'prescription' (Burke 1790). Burke assumes values are adopted because they are generally useful, or, to put it another way, that they are *functional*. He refers to 'the wisdom of nations and of ages'. There is an element of truth in this, but there are important reservations to make. Values do not always emerge through practice and experience, but in packages – like, for example, Calvinism (see Tawney 1926) – which initially stand and fall as a whole. Calvinism emphasized a work ethic, the principle that 'if any will not work, nor shall he eat' – which can be seen as functional at a certain period in history. The doctrine was (and arguably still is) particularly important in Britain. Societies change, and values that used to be functional can become in later periods *dysfunctional*, or negative in their effects – like the subservient role of women or the encouragement of childbirth. Values which are functional for some people are not necessarily functional for others. Chapter 1 made out an argument that people's interests diverge. The case that social values are partial – favouring some interests rather than others – is strongly put by Marxists. When Marx railed against 'bourgeois' morality he clearly considered that the moral order favoured the bourgeoisie as the dominant class in society. Respect for property, for example, must work for the benefit of those who have property against those who do not. Functionalist ideas tend to depend on a consensus view of social values; Marxism, by contrast, emphasizes the conflicts between them. (The Marxist case is considered in more detail in Chapter 8.)

The fact that morals are socially defined does not mean that everyone in the society thinks they are right, or even that most people do. There are often complex variations in people's opinions. Take, for example, the case of abortion. There are those who think abortion is murder; others accept that it is a form of killing but think it is legitimate in extreme cases, like pregnancy after rape; some think it is justified to prevent the birth of a child who would be handicapped; some think it is justified if it would cause undue hardship to the woman to have the child; while many feminists argue for abortion on demand, because a woman has a right to choose what can be done with her body. For the purposes of the argument, assume that these five opinions are spread equally through society. Then a majority of people would think that there is some moral reason for denying people abortions; but a majority would also think there is a moral ground for permitting abortion. This would not be because there was any consensus or middle view. There are at least four norms – one protecting the interests of the mother, one protecting the interests of the child, the norm that killing is wrong, and the view that some lives are worth less than others – which are in conflict with each other and which can be balanced in different ways. No single answer genuinely reflects 'majority opinion' in such a case; there are only different resolutions of the conflict.

In social policy, explicit value conflicts do occur, but many of the most prominent debates concern issues – like abortion or sexuality – which are of marginal importance in relation to issues of welfare provision. Many more decisions are made within an accepted framework of moral values. This does not mean that the actions of policy-makers are explicitly moral; policies are motivated by many factors, including for example self-interest, political convenience, and economic constraints. The effect of norms is more subtle; it is to constrain decision-making about social policy and define the options which are available. This is most obvious in the extreme cases: some policies are simply unthinkable. Jonathan Swift once made a 'modest proposal' that the way to solve the Irish famine was to eat babies – a point he intended to remind government that they could not behave as if moral responsibilities did not apply. But there are many other policies besides which are based in a taken-for-granted view of society; the impact of social values is less obvious but no less pervasive. There is, for example, a high moral value placed on 'the family'. Child care is generally organized on the principle that care in a family is a good thing and care outside a family is not. Freeman argues that the frequent moves common in residential care and the lack of consistent relationships mar children's personal development (Freeman 1983). They lack stimulation and are not given the chance to acquire independence and a sense of responsibility. There is, he writes, 'every possibility that the development of children in care may become stunted or distorted. Everything possible, accordingly, should be done to keep children whenever possible out of care. . . . Children have the moral right not to be in care' (ibid.: 148, 150). This may seem, at first, a realistic argument based on a practical assessment of children's welfare. But the interpretation of the problem has been made within a framework of expectations about 'normal' family relationships. If children in institutions fail to develop as other children do, it may be because of the problems and deprivations which led to them coming into care in the first place. If institutional care is failing to provide a stable, stimulating environment, this may have as much to do with the organization of the institutions, and persistent attempts to move children back into 'families', as with any fundamental flaw in the concept of the institution. One does not hear arguments that children's development is distorted or stunted if they go to Eton; but Eton is also a residential institution. The construction of the problem – the idea that the alternative has to be seen in terms of substitute family care rather than better institutions – is a normative issue, not simply a practical one; the interpretation is socially determined.

POLICIES FOR WOMEN

In a number of ways social services reinforce social norms. An illustration is the emphasis in social policy on the traditional role of women – or, to be more precise, not so much the 'traditional' role as an idealized norm. The education system has been accused of imposing stereotypes of gender roles – both formally, by channelling girls into particular subjects and areas of study, and informally, through the kinds of social contact fostered in schools, the stress on certain values – like discipline and obedience – and preparation for 'family life', which may be implicit as well as explicit in the school curriculum. (These arguments are summarized in Finch 1984.) Health visitors have many responsibilities for 'health education' in general, but the primary work is to supervise new mothers with babies to make sure the mother looks after the baby properly. Both policies could be said to be working within a widely accepted system of values. If social services fail to challenge social norms, there is little to explain; the services reflect the society of which they are a part. Equally, however, they can be seen as complementing and reinforcing a particular view of the role of women.

In social security, there is an assumption that women are likely to be dependent on husbands. The Beveridge Report established a special class of contributions for married women, with limited entitlement to benefit because of their dependent status – though there was also the relative advantage that women whose husbands died were entitled to widows benefits (Beveridge 1942). Some benefits contained, until recently, openly discriminatory provisions to limit women's entitlement to benefit. Invalid Care Allowance, for the carers of severely disabled people, was barred to married women until a case in the European court overturned the rule. The Non-Contributory Invalidity Pension, introduced in 1975, was introduced to help people who did not qualify for National Insurance; but it was at first refused to married women. Married women became entitled only two years later, subject to a special condition: they must be substantially impaired in their ability to perform household duties. After a further year it was apparently decided that this rule was too generous, and the regulations were tightened up; married women were only able to claim if they were unable to perform household duties to any substantial extent. The difference appears to be slight, but it had a major effect; a woman who was able to do half the housework would be entitled before the change, but would not be after it. Most of these provisions have now been struck out under pressure from the European Community.

There is also, in social security policy, a 'cohabitation rule': a woman who lives with a man and has a sexual relationship with him is often assumed on that basis alone to rely on him financially. The rule is worth considering in a little more detail. A couple who are 'living together as man and wife' are taken as sharing financial resources if they are members of the same household; if the relationship is a stable one; if they have children; if they share finances; if they have a sexual relationship; or if their relationship is like that of husband and wife in other (undefined) ways. Although officers are instructed not to ask about sexual relationships, sex is central to the issue; a brother and sister, or a parent with an adult child, would not be treated as 'cohabiting' even though the other criteria besides a sexual relationship and having a child together all applied. (This can, by the way, lead to some absurdly coy interviewing.)

In moral terms, the cohabitation rule has some curious implications. For example, it reduces benefit for people who form a stable sexual relationship but imposes no penalty for promiscuity. Phillips (1981), in an outstanding essay on Aid to Families with Dependent Children (a benefit in the United States for single mothers on low incomes), makes a number of points about benefits for single parents which apply to this rule. If considered from the point of view of financial incentives, the rule discourages mothers from remarriage, or from entering a relationship which is likely to lead to remarriage; it discourages the fathers from child support; it discourages the mothers from allowing people not on benefit to live with the household; it encourages mothers to put out the fathers; it encourages, then, small family units who are less able to support the child. She is doubtful that these incentives make very much difference in practice, but the point that emerges is an important one; the system is not designed simply to enforce moral principles in any obvious way.

The rule applied in the United Kingdom is not discriminatory in itself, because it can be used against male claimants as well as female claimants; but in practice it seems to be used mainly against single parents, the vast majority of whom are women and who are considered prime candidates for investigation. The rule could, then, be considered to be a form of 'institutional sexism' – sexist in effect if not in form. But this begs the question, whether it is the rule which has the effect or whether it only reflects a more fundamental problem. Without the cohabitation rule it is not possible to have a benefit for single parents – because the difference between single parents and couples is the absence of the other parent. The social security system begins with the situation that currently exists, in which women are primarily responsible for child care, child care limits ability to work, when women work it tends to be in low-paid jobs with little or no prospect of advancement, and the main earners in the household tend to be male. The root of the problem is not so much the way in which benefits are paid, as is the case with a large number of women who have sole responsibility for child care without financial independence; and the issue can be resolved only by removing the sources of disadvantage, for example by removing the responsibility for child care or by giving all carers a household wage to make them independent. In effect, the assumption of dependency is justified by the fact that many women are dependent – but the assumption in the service also helps to bring about the situation in reality, because a woman whose benefit is stopped may be forced to appeal to the man for financial support.

There is a dilemma for the social services. In many families women are financially dependent on men, and they have primary responsibility for child care. These circumstances are supported by fairly strong moral codes; it would be unrealistic to ignore the way many people live, and it could have undesirable consequences (e.g. by undermining the case for extra support for single parents). Equally, there is a powerful feminist argument to the contrary: these policies force people into a particular mould; acceptance of these social conditions as given, when women are at a substantial disadvantage, is likely to make their disadvantage permanent. There is no ethically neutral position.

MORAL REJECTION

The reinforcement of social norms generally requires the definition of boundaries. Moral norms prompt moral judgements; the same kind of codes which cause some actions to be valued, also roughly define the limits beyond which behaviour is unacceptable. A person who is in breach of moral norms is said to be *deviant*. It should be clear, from the definition of norms given before, that deviance does not mean that a person is simply different from others or even that a person is socially rejected. It means that there are rules which have been broken (Cohen 1966: 36). There are many explanations for the process by which deviants are marked off from the rest of society. They are mainly concerned with criminality, which leads to the discussion of areas outside welfare provision; but there are also aspects of theories of deviance which relate directly to the receipt of welfare.

The idea of 'deviance' is dichotomous – it is presented as if there were hardly any grey areas and people fell clearly on one side of the border or another. It is not possible to be half a thief or a bit of an unmarried mother – though in reality, the distinction between 'moral' and 'immoral' actions is rarely clear-cut. The principle of *less eligibility* under the Poor Law was an attempt to preserve a distinction between the people who receive welfare and those who do not. The idea, according to *The Poor Law Report of 1834*, was that the position of the person on relief, the 'pauper', 'on the whole shall not be made really or apparently so eligible as the situation of the independent labourer of the lowest class' (Checkland and Checkland 1974: 335). This was not solely a moral distinction: it owed a certain amount, too, to the economic beliefs of the time, and Ricardo's 'Iron Law of Wages', which suggested that poor relief might undermine the wages of those who were working. But the condition of many independent labourers was so bad that it was virtually impossible to make the circumstances of paupers any worse, and the maintenance of 'less eligibility' came to depend in large part on moral attitudes and the 'stigma' of pauperism. The doctrine survives in the concern that people should not be 'better off on the dole'. This is interpreted to mean, not that individuals should not be better off when not working – which is what one should expect if the issue was one of 'incentives to work' – but that no-one should be better off on social security than people in low-paid jobs.

Despite the attempt to draw dividing lines between categories of people, things in practice are rather more complicated. Lemert distinguishes *primary deviants* – people who have done something bad – from *secondary deviants*, who are 'bad people' (Lemert 1951). The difference, he suggests, is a matter of the *label* attached to deviance; a secondary deviant is distinguished from the rest of the community and is likely to be isolated and rejected. Labelling theory, extending Lemert's argument, argues that people are deviant because they are defined as deviant by society. Becker writes that 'Social groups create deviance by making the rules whose infraction constitutes deviance' (Becker 1963: 9). The label is defined by the social rule, not by the behaviour of the person. To put it another way, deviance is created by society, not by the individual deviants.

Social services may identify people as deviant by labelling them. A person becomes 'mentally ill' when a doctor diagnoses the complaint; a family is a 'problem family' when an agency says it is. The value of labelling theory has been to prompt caution in the uses of labels like this, because of the negative effects they can have on recipients. Phillips found, in a survey of attitudes, that a normal individual who had visited a psychiatrist, or worse been in a psychiatric hospital, was likely to be rejected by others, in some cases more than people whose behaviour was disturbed but who had not sought any help (Phillips 1966). The labelling perspective points to the role that services may play in identifying people as deviant, and helps to explain why people may be reluctant to put themselves in that position. But it would be a mistake to overestimate its importance: in the case of mental illness, the evidence is that it is the behaviour of mentally ill people, not the label, which is the main factor leading to social rejection (see Segal 1978: 213).

The receipt of welfare may itself be taken as evidence of some moral deficiency. Certain classes of recipient have been seen as pathologically immoral – in other words, there is something in their personal make-up which makes them different from other people and explains why they behave immorally. Promiscuous women and unmarried mothers were treated in the past as 'moral defectives' (a term used in the 1913 Mental Deficiency Act, abolished in 1959) and committed to mental institutions, where some of them are still living now. Another example is the 'problem family'. 'Problem families' are not the same thing as 'families with problems'; the term means that they create problems for social agencies. Blacker, in a pamphlet prepared for the Eugenics Society, picks out the 'commonly recognized' features: mental subnormality, temperamental instability, ineducability, a squalid home, and the presence of numerous children (Blacker 1952). In other words, they are dirty, stupid, violent people who breed like rabbits. Spencer describes them as large, transient, and socially isolated (Spencer 1963). They are likely to be chronically dependent on social services, exploitative, and fail to respond to the help they do receive. This kind of description is now out of fashion in writing on social work, but the main text on housing management in Britain still contains the following advice:

> No reorganisation of administration, no application of technical skill, can guarantee good results in the community's efforts to convert the small group who form the hard core of problem families into tolerably decent citizens. . . . Apart from a few borderline cases, all these problem families exhibit one common factor, namely, their inability to cope with their circumstances. . . . One or the other of the parents may be the victim of longstanding mental or physical ill-health which can never be wholly relieved. In some few instances, one or both of the parents may apparently be physically well and of average intelligence, but of a type which the average man in the street would classify as "bone idle". This type of individual is only too pleased to welcome a succession of welfare visitors and psychiatric social workers and to keep them stringing along while he evades his responsibilities.
>
> (Macey 1982: 433, 436)

The author suggests that

> anything which brands the family as a "problem family" ought to be strenuously avoided. Nevertheless, it may sometimes be desirable to move a family from a good post-war dwelling to a less desirable one and to "promote" them to better accommodation as they respond to persuasion.
>
> (*ibid.*: 437)

The idea that people who are 'unable to cope' will respond to persuasion by being moved to worse housing rests on the basic premise that they have some choice about their circumstances – almost a contradiction in terms.

The assumption that welfare recipients are likely to be immoral depends in part on the attribution of some responsibility for their condition. According to Merton, a person who rejects the values and structure of society is likely to 'retreat' from it. 'Retreatists' include 'psychotics, autists, pariahs, outcasts, vagrants, vagabonds, tramps, chronic drunkards and drug addicts' (Merton 1968: 194). There are certain problems with this argument. There is no reason to suppose that a 'drunkard' or 'vagrant' rejects social attitudes; Merton assumes people choose to be like this. People can reject some values and not others; Merton assumes it is all or nothing. And 'social values' are inconsistent. 'Drunkards' to some people are 'hard-drinking men' to others; mentally ill people are seen as being in need of help, but they are treated as deviant if they actually take it (Phillips 1963). Welfare recipients are caught between conflicting social codes.

Part of the professional code of social workers is that they should not be 'judgemental' – a term which means, not that they should not make judgements, but that they should not reject people or hold them in contempt on moralistic grounds. On the face of it, the treatment of social-service recipients as deviant seems to be a simple contradiction of principles of welfare. But the position is more complex than this, because the same kinds of norm which define welfare as a moral activity may establish expectations about the type of claimant and the sort of service that should be given. People are labelled, or marked out as deviant, by the very fact of claiming welfare. They may be assumed to have chosen their dependent position, and stigmatized morally as a result. The process of distinguishing the 'deserving' and the 'undeserving' poor can be seen as a fundamental part of the process of welfare provision. This issue is examined further in the next chapter.

III

Altruism, exchange, and
stigma

Summary: *Some moral behaviour is altruistic, based in concern for others. But there are also norms of reciprocity, making a return for things received, and people who fail to make a return are likely to be rejected or stigmatized.*

Stigma is a complex idea, including the attributes and feelings of the stigmatized person and the attitudes of others. There are physical and mental stigmas, moral stigmas, stigmas of poverty and dependency. The rejection of welfare recipients can spoil ideals of an altruistic society.

A number of moral principles imply duties to give to others. Feinberg outlines several (Feinberg 1980, Ch. 6). They include, for example, indebtedness, where one person owes something to another; commitment, where a duty is owed to a third party (like the duty of a trustee to the object of a charity); and reparation, when one person has to compensate another for harm done. There are duties owed within families or according to status. These are specific moral duties, dependent on a particular context. But there are also a number of other duties which are general, or 'humanitarian', because they are owed to everyone (like giving to charity), or the duty to meet people's basic needs.

Titmuss emphasized the importance of *ultra obligations*, behaviour which depended not on obligations to particular people but on a general sense of moral principle (Titmuss 1970: 212). This provided the basis for a model of welfare which would unite society as a whole. For Titmuss, the 'good society' was one in which it was possible for people to give, one which relied more on the 'social market' than the economic market. Boulding suggests, in a passage approved by Titmuss, that 'we can identify the "grant" or unilateral transfer . . . as the distinguishing mark of the social just as exchange or bilateral transfer is a mark of the economic' (Boulding 1973: 193). The 'social market' refers to a network of non-economic relationships between individuals, families, groups, and communities. Titmuss's ideal was a society founded on *altruism* or concern for others rather than oneself. The provision of welfare does not depend exclusively on altruism; it is also a question of social organization. Sugden points out that the case for a national health service, for example, is a form of rational collective action, not a replacement of private provision by a surfeit of goodwill (Sugden 1980). Altruism can, unaided, be rather a haphazard way to provide services. There is little link between the extent of need and the willingness of people to donate. Lyall points out that whereas, for example, there are ten times as many deaf people in Britain as blind, they get only a seventh of the cash (Lyall 1980). And, as a former director of MIND, the National Association for Mental Health, complained, 'the mentally ill do not have the instant appeal of the furry, feathered and four-footed' (quoted in Lyall 1980). Gifts to charity depend on a number of factors, including traditions of giving, its appeal to fundraisers, and the distribution of resources among donors.

The activities of the 'voluntary sector' in welfare represent an important part of welfare provision as a whole. Jones and his colleagues give a valuable summary of the scope and limitations of the work (Jones, Brown and Bradshaw 1978). The type of work done is extremely varied, including direct service-giving – two-thirds of it, according to the Wolfenden Report, in personal social services; running 'voluntary organizations' (which may be professionally staffed); participating in self-help groups; fundraising; and activity as pressure groups. The work they do is often valuable – creating diversity of provision, assisting state services, doing some things which state-run services can't do effectively (like helping drug addicts), filling in gaps in services, helping to inform people about services, experimenting with new types of provision, and sometimes criticizing the way in which the state services act. But there are also problems: the services are not necessarily provided in the places where they are needed; voluntary services can outlast their usefulness, after the state has taken on the responsibility; volunteers are not always willing to do necessary but dull work, like administration; the voluntary workers may be badly trained, have unsuitable attitudes towards clients, or the wrong type of motivation for helping. In fairness, many of these criticisms could also be levelled at 'professional' services, and the contribution made by the voluntary sector is substantial; the Wolfenden Commission (1977) estimated that voluntary effort was equivalent, in Britain, to perhaps 400,000 full-time workers.

In attempting to understand why and when people attempt to help, it is interesting to refer to the psychological literature on *prosocial behaviour* (a term intended to be the opposite of 'antisocial' behaviour). The reasons why people give are complex. Wright outlines a number of explanations (Wright 1971, Ch. 6). One is biological, that altruism is instinctive or inborn. Another is that altruism is prompted by attachment, or an emotional bond. Both of these help to explain why people should be altruistic to others they are close to – like parents to children – but not why people should help strangers. Psychological explanations are that they may feel sympathy towards them, identify emotionally ('empathize'), or project their own feelings about the other person's circumstances. Gerard suggests, from survey evidence, that volunteers are more likely than others to have a positive view of their fellow humans, to have a religious commitment, and to put less emphasis on the material aspects of life (Gerard 1985). Behaviourists may interpret helping behaviour as a learnt, 'conditioned response', for which people have been rewarded in the past. Wright's other explanations are social: people may be prompted to give by the example of others; they may be conforming to social norms, or acting out of a sense of duty. Gerard emphasizes social motives of *beneficence*, that is a compassionate and moral response to the needs of others, and *solidarity*, that is identification and 'fraternity' with those who are deprived.

Titmuss's research was based in an examination of blood donation, an area he chose because it represented a service which could be done either through organized altruism or through the economic market. He came to the conclusion that not only was it morally better to donate blood but that the quantity and quality of blood obtained was better than in systems, like the US, where blood is paid for. Pinker complains that blood donation is not a very good example of altruistic behaviour, because it involves no real cost to the donor; but the results from Titmuss's survey are still interesting as a guide to people's motivation. He classifies them, broadly, as follows:

(1) Altruism: 26.4 per cent of answers.
    'Knowing I mite be saving somebody's life' (*sic*)
    'Anonymously, without financial reward, to help others'
    'No man is an island'
    'I get my surgical shoes through the NHS. This is some slight
    return and I want to help people.'
(2) Gratitude for good health: 1.4 per cent of answers.
    'To me it is a form of thanking God for my own good health'
(3) Reciprocity: 9.8 per cent of answers.
    'Some unknown person gave blood to save my wife's life'
    'I have a motor bike and someday I may need blood to help me'
(4) Replacement: 0.8 per cent of answers.
    'My mother was a blood donor . . . when she died in 1958 I
    decided to carry on in her place'
(5) Awareness of need for blood: 6.4 per cent of answers.
    'After seeing a bad accident I thought it was the best way I
    could help'
(6) Duty: 3.5 per cent of answers.
    'Sense of duty to the community and nation as a whole'
(7) Rare blood group: 1.1 per cent of answers.
(8) To obtain some benefit: 1.8 per cent of answers.
    'Since I became a donor I have not had a single nose bleed'
    'Snob appeal'
(9) Miscellaneous: 5 per cent of answers.
    'To get a good cup of tea'
    'No money to spare. Plenty of blood to spare'

                                                    (Titmuss 1970)
(Titmuss also mentions that other replies included response to
appeals, especially from the war effort or the defence services. There
were also a few giving many reasons.)

Titmuss's classification of reasons seems fairly arbitrary. Answers
like 'snob appeal' or 'to get a good cup of tea' may well conceal
altruistic motives; on the other hand, the answer 'I get my surgical
shoes from the NHS' seems to show a desire to make a return for
services received, rather than altruism.

There does seem to be a strong sense in many of these answers that
giving blood is a form of exchange rather than a gift. Alchian and
Allen argue that even if people ᵤnly get a feeling of self-satisfaction,

they are getting some return from altruistic behaviour, and so that giving is not essentially different from other (economic) types of exchange (Alchian and Allen 1973). But the idea that people who give are somehow getting some return from it seems rather to spoil the idea of 'altruism' – as if to say that people are all selfish really. Weale suggests, I think rightly, that there is a moral difference between this kind of *internal* gain and an *external* gain or reward (Weale 1983, Ch. 2).

RECIPROCITY

Ultra obligations, Titmuss suggests, imply no expectation that the person who gives or helps will get something back for what is done. But there is, in most if not all societies, a general obligation to make some return for things received. This is called the *norm of reciprocity*, or *exchange*.

The idea of 'exchange' does not always mean that the person who receives has got to be the one who makes a return. This is called *restricted* or *balanced* exchange. There is also *generalized* exchange, where the return goes not necessarily to the person who has given but to others again who will give in their turn – like the people who gave blood because they had once received it or because they might need it themselves. Lévi-Strauss, the anthropologist, extends the idea of 'generalized' exchange to include almost any gift, because a circle of exchange could be completed. Generalized exchange, he writes, 'establishes a system of operations conducted "on credit" ' (Lévi-Strauss 1949: 265). The norm of reciprocity creates, then, a basic justification for a collectivist view of moral responsibility, one which depends on social rules rather than the decisions of individuals. The classic example of this from anthropology is the 'Kula Ring', a formal exchange of essentially worthless articles by the Trobriand islanders, which islanders had to join in to avoid social rejection (Mauss 1925, Ch. 2). In contemporary social welfare, the best example is probably the recognition of responsibilities to old people. If old people gain their entitlements by what they did for their elders, their successors are morally bound whether or not they have chosen to be. Another example is the organization in the United Kingdom of state pensions. Pensions are paid for on a 'pay as you go' system, from the taxes and

Figure 3.1 The advantages of exchange

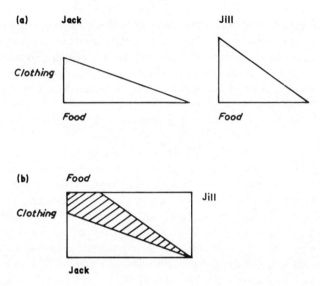

contributions of people who are currently earning. The people who are paying for pensioners now will have their pensions paid by those who are still earning when they retire – not, it should be noted, by their own contributions. When the Labour government in 1969 proposed a scheme offering increased pensions in twenty years' time – a pattern incorporated in the 1975 State Earnings-Related Pension Scheme, 'SERPS' – *New Society* attacked it as immoral, promising ourselves bigger pensions at our children's expense while refusing to pay for our parents now (*New Society* 1969).

Part of the reason for the general acceptance of a principle of reciprocity rests in the economic advantages to be gained from exchange. By exchange, people can specialize in producing some articles while the people they exchange with produce others. This can lead both parties to be better off than before the exchange. This can be formally demonstrated in a set of diagrams (Fig. 3.1). Assume that two people, Jack and Jill, are able by themselves to produce a certain amount of clothing or food for themselves, and the more they produce of one, the less they are able to produce of the other. This gives each of them a limit, or 'production possibility frontier' (Fig. 3.1a). If they specialize and then exchange their goods, between them, they can produce more than either of them can do separately. In Figure 3.1b Jill has been turned upside down on Jack. The result is that both of them can get more out of it than they would trying to do things by themselves. Neither of them, alone, could have anything from the shaded area. Together they can go beyond their individual frontiers. If reciprocity is a norm, one explanation is that it is part of a process which is useful to all the parties.

This is called, in economics, the theory of *comparative advantage*. There are two main reservations to make in applying it to social theory. One is that different societies specialize to differing degrees; as a general rule, there is more interdependence in industrialized societies. The second is what you specialize in affects your position socially; a division of labour in the home, with women specializing in some activities and men in others, may be economically rational but socially oppressive.

Exchange has been strongly linked with status. Simmel suggests that a person who is unable to reciprocate is made to feel gratitude, increasing the esteem of the donor at his own expense (Simmel 1950: 393). Homans develops this basic idea into a full-blown theory of social behaviour. A person who does something which is valuable to others gains esteem. This esteem carries with it 'authority', or influence, over others (Homans 1961: 288). The person who gives gains esteem, and with it status and power; the person who receives, conversely, loses them. The implications for the recipients of social services – services which are to some degree defined by the dependency of their clients – are clear.

Homans's theory is mainly concerned with the behaviour of people in small groups, though Blau extends it to deal with people in the wider society (Blau 1964). The main limitations of the theory are, first, that it overlooks the importance of generalized exchange, and second, that it cannot explain status which is traditional (or *ascribed*) rather than earned (or *acquired*). In the context of welfare, though, it offers an interesting insight into what happens in the course of the 'welfare exchange'. The idea that recipients should make some contribution for what they receive is central to many systems of welfare. The principle of social insurance – paying contributions to protect against sickness and old age – is used in societies as different as those of the United States and the Soviet Union.

'All social services', Pinker argues, 'are systems of exchange' (Pinker 1971: 153). Even where there is no formal mechanism like insurance, the idea of 'contribution' may be important. Children may be protected either because their parents have contributed on their behalf or because they are likely to contribute in the future. Old people may be considered to have contributed through their lifetime. But a recipient of welfare who has not made a contribution, and who is not likely to make one in the future – like someone who is long-term unemployed – is likely to receive an inferior, stigmatized service.

Welfare exchanges, Uttley writes, can be based on three different kinds of principle (Uttley 1980). They can be based on 'beneficence', or charity. They can be based in rights, and here the effect will depend on whether those rights are earned (like rights to insurance benefits or pensions) or donated (like welfare benefits). Third, there are a number of welfare provisions which can be seen to offer welfare as a return for the benefit to society. There are compensatory services, like Industrial Disablement Benefit or War Pensions. There are promotive services, like education, which are considered to offer as much to the wider society as to the individual receiving them. And there are control-orientated services, like social casework, which aim to get the individual to change in order to receive the benefits of membership of society.

Welfare exchanges are not, then, a simple trade of humiliation for service, even if this is a part of the process at times. But many of the exchanges involved are likely to involve a loss of status. Although the principle of the gift seems to bind society together, it can also divide recipients from the rest. This paradox is explained by Sahlins (1974, Ch. 5). He describes three kinds of reciprocity: generalized, balanced, and negative. Generalized exchange occurs when people give without expecting something in return, in the belief that others would, or will, do the same for them. It is most often found in intimate relationships, like families. Balanced exchange is strictly reciprocal, the exchange between more distant friends of business

partners. Negative exchange is self-seeking and competitive. Exchange determines social distance: if our exchange is generalized, we
know that we are close; if negative, we are not.

It follows that there is a distance between the people who are able
to exchange with others on equal terms and those who have little or
nothing to offer in return. Redistribution between rich and poor
brings the poor into society: 'The greater the wealth gap . . . the
greater the demonstrable assistance that is necessary to maintain a
given degree of sociability' (Sahlins 1974: 211). This means that
charity, or something very like it, is necessary to hold society
together. But when it happens, the governing principle is not
altruism, but negative exchange: 'The collectivity, of which the poor
person is a part, enters into a relationship with him, treating him as
an object' (Simmel 1908: 31). In other words, poor people receive
charity, but they are rejected as a result. The social services carry a
stigma.

It was on this basis that Pinker challenged Titmuss's argument for
a good society. Titmuss recognized the elements of reciprocity in his
own work on blood donation. 'There is in all these transactions', he
wrote, 'an unspoken assumption of some gift-reciprocity; that those
who give as members of society to strangers will themselves (or their
families) eventually benefit as members of that society' (Pinker 1970:
243). He argued that this supported the case for an altruistic society –
or, perhaps more accurately, a society based on generosity, the
behaviour of people ready to help. His ideal of a society bound
together by a 'gift relationship' is ruined if the people who receive
help are stigmatized and rejected by those who give it. If Pinker is
right about the effect of reciprocity, Titmuss is wrong.

STIGMA

The stigma which results from dependency on welfare is a major
factor in welfare provision; Pinker refers to it as the central issue in
social policy (Pinker 1971: 136). But it is a complex issue, which raises
many more problems than reciprocity (see Spicker 1984; the
argument of this section is drawn from that book).

Stigma can mean, in the first place, an attribute of the stigmatized
person. Goffman refers to stigma as:

a failing, a shortcoming, a handicap
(Goffman 1963: 12)

an attribute that is deeply discrediting
(*ibid.*: 13)

an attribute which makes (the stigmatized person) different from
others . . . and of less desirable kind
(*ibid.*: 12)

a shameful differentness
(*ibid.*: 21)

However, unless stigma is seen solely as an individual, pathological
problem, the stigma is discrediting because of the social construction
that is put on it. Stigma, a 'stain on one's good name', may also result
from the attitudes of other people. Rejection, loss of esteem, and
discrimination are all referred to, at different times, as 'stigma'.
Goffman suggests that a stigma 'is really a special kind of relationship
between attribute and stereotype' (*ibid.*: 14). This probably overstates
the importance of personal characteristics; people can be stigmatized
because of what others believe to be true, even though it may not be.

Third, stigma can refer to the feelings of the stigmatized person.
Scott, for example, writes, 'The blind person comes to feel that he is
not completely accepted as a mature, responsible person. As a
second-class citizen, he must deal with the sense of inadequacy that
inevitably accompanies that status' (Scott 1969: 37). This is often
specifically related to the reaction of the people who receive services
and benefits, and feel reluctant to claim, ashamed, or humiliated as a
result. Thirty per cent of people eligible for Supplementary Benefit
(Income Support), and nearly half of those entitled to claim Family
Income Supplement (Family Credit), do not receive the benefits they
should. This is frequently attributed to stigma, though ignorance
about benefits, the low value of some benefits, and the problems of
claiming also play a large part; stigma is more properly taken into
account, Weisbrod argues, as a cost that people have to bear in order
to receive benefits, even if it does not actually prevent them from
claiming (Weisbrod 1970: 7).

These three elements – the attributes of stigmatized people, their
feelings, and the attitudes of others – all contribute to the idea of
stigma; they are difficult to separate in practice. The 'stigma of

poverty', for example, may mean that the person is poor (which is an attribute, and perhaps a shortcoming); that the person is socially rejected, because of poverty; and possibly, that the poverty leads to a sense of shame, failure, or degradation. There are many attributes which might be seen as stigmatizing. First, there are *physical stigmas* – including illness, disability and old age. People are rejected because of negative reactions to their physical features. There are *mental stigmas*, like mental illness, mental handicap, and addiction. Like physical stigmas, they can cause fear or a sense of personal threat, but they can also be associated with the perception of behaviour as immoral or disruptive. The *stigmas of poverty* include unemployment, living in slums, low income, and homelessness. Poor people are rejected as inadequate, dependent, feckless, and work-shy. There are *stigmas of dependency* in themselves – including dependency on social services – which make poverty or disability worse. And lastly, there are *moral stigmas* – rejection attached to the breach of moral norms discussed in the previous chapter.

In practice, these stigmas overlap, not only because people who are physically or mentally stigmatized are likely to be poor and dependent, but because the effect of a stigma is to obliterate other features of a personality, leading to treatment of stigmatized people as if they fell wholly on the other side of a border. Stigmatized people are, in other words, treated as deviant, as if they were outside the moral order of society. They are not in an identical social position; there are important distinctions made between them, not least the distinctions they make themselves. Old and disabled people have in general a higher status than unemployed men or unmarried mothers. At the same time, there is a barrier which separates them from the rest of society – a boundary, division, or social distance.

The process by which this happens is complex. The assumptions made about stigmatized people are often difficult to justify. Physically or mentally disordered people do not have to be seen as threatening; they are not necessarily dependent. Poor people are not necessarily immoral, but poverty is commonly associated with immorality, as if people should be blamed for their poverty. The association made between different kinds of stigma is itself irrational. Stigma depends, in large part, on prejudice.

Prejudice, however, is based in the same kinds of social norms which underlie morals. The term 'prejudice', as Burke points out, has positive as well as negative aspects. People act morally, not because they carefully think through every moral issue, but because they are disposed to it by their socialization. He writes:

Prejudice is of ready application in the emergency; it previously engages the mind in a steady course of wisdom and virtue, and does not leave the man hesitating of decision, sceptical, puzzled and unresolved. Prejudice renders a man's virtue his habit; and not a series of unconnected acts. Through just prejudice, his duty becomes his nature.

(Burke 1790: 105–6)

There is a fundamental social process at work here. Physical and mental differences breach expectations, or norms, and incur prejudice. Poverty, dependency, and moral stigmas also breach social norms; they are expectations of different kinds, but they are structured through socialization in the same way, and the response tends to be similar – loss of esteem, low status, and social rejection.

The effect of this, in the most extreme cases, is an accumulation of different kinds of stigmas. Single homeless people are likely to be poor and isolated simply by virtue of their condition. Many are also ill. In a government survey, 30 per cent of single homeless people complained of physical illness, 10 per cent reported mental illness or mental handicap, 8 per cent mentioned physical handicap, and 3 per cent alcoholism (Drake, O'Brien, and Biebuyck 1981: 36). The existence of problems of this type leads to stereotyping about homeless people as a group. The homeless man, Bahr writes,

is, or is perceived as being, defective physically (scarred, handicapped, aged and diseased), mentally (psychotic, senile, or manifesting bizarre symptoms), morally (a pervert, criminal or addict), psychologically (low self-esteem, high self-aggression), socially (disaffiliated), legally (treated by police and courts as a resident of an occupied country rather than as a free man), economically (impoverished, unemployed), and ecologically (he resides in a neighbourhood in which no 'decent person' would live).

(Bahr 1973: 120–1)

There may be some foundation for these stigmas, but their scope extends far beyond what can be justified by the situation. Many single homeless people are also young and healthy; 8 per cent have been in higher education; almost half are in work (Drake *et al.*, 1981). What is wrong with them is that they have nowhere to live.

The problem of stigma represents a fundamental challenge to ideals of solidarity, beneficence, or ultra obligations, because it implies that people are likely to be rejected socially even when they are supported materially by others in the community. This may substantially limit the scope of social services to increase individual and social well-being through the 'social market'.

IV

Freedom

Summary: *The concept of freedom means that a person is free from restraint ('negative freedom') to do something ('positive freedom'), and is able to make the choice ('psychological freedom'); in practice these ideas are inseparable. The idea of individual freedom depends on a view of people as rational, autonomous actors; an alternative view is social, seeing freedom in terms of relationships between people.*

Paternalism, or intervention for someone's own good, may be seen as a breach of individual freedom; but it may be justified either to increase a person's power to choose, or on other moral criteria.

Welfare depends in large part on people's choices and preferences. Personal freedom has been represented as a primary social value, and a 'welfare interest' because it is seen as one of the most important ways in which welfare can be achieved. But the concept of 'personal freedom' is an ambiguous one. There are three main concepts included in it. The first is *negative freedom*, which is the absence of coercion. Coercion is described by Isaiah Berlin as 'the deliberate interference of other human beings within the area in which I could act' (Berlin 1969: 122). People's freedom is limited when they are interfered with – for example, when they are visited by a social worker or when they are required to go to school. This does not mean that a person who takes this view of freedom disagrees with the idea of social work or of sending children to school; it means that there is a price to pay for doing so, and any infringement of freedom implied by these actions has to be justified on the basis of other values.

Second, there is *positive freedom*, which may be understood as the power to act as one chooses. This implies, not just the absence of constraint, but the capacity to act. Take the case of a boy – call him Alan – who is severely handicapped and unable to move or speak. He lives in an institution, and is looked after by care staff who work to their own routine. Alan is fed, cleaned, and clothed, efficiently, at regular times. Is he free? In the negative sense of 'freedom', he is still free, because he is not being coerced, prevented from doing anything, or interfered with 'within the area in which he could act'. In the positive sense of freedom, he is not free, because he is unable to exercise any choices.

The third view of freedom is *psychological freedom*. This implies the ability to choose. Alan, or the unwilling school-child, may lack the ability to choose, because they cannot think independently for themselves; by the idea of psychological freedom, they would be unfree. Alan may be able to gain a degree of freedom through persistent attempts at communication and education, and an emphasis on psychological freedom would call for this. Similarly, one of the purposes of insisting that children go to school is to equip them to make choices – giving them the power to act.

The idea of psychological freedom is sometimes confused with positive freedom (e.g. by Berlin, in his famous essay 'Two Concepts of Liberty', 1969), but they are quite discrete. The difference between them is that although a person might have the power to act, the ability to choose may itself be unfree – like the behaviour of the drug addict whose will is sapped by his addiction. Imagine, further, that Alan has a brilliant mind. He absorbs everything around him, is able to create poems and stories, and has a rich and varied inner life. By the positive concept of freedom, he is still not free, because he lacks the power to act – and worse, has even less power to do as he might choose. But by the concept of psychological freedom, he may well be thought of as 'free', because he is free to make choices.

Freedom, according to Berlin, depends on the number of options a person has, how accessible each option is, and on the relative importance of different opportunities to the person's life (*ibid.*: p.xxxix). The fewer a person's choices, and the harder they are, the more vulnerable a person is to 'coercion'. It is important which opportunities they have: as Taylor points out, traffic lights are an infringement of freedom too, but they are just not very important in deciding whether someone is 'free' or not (Taylor 1979). The real issue in negative freedom is how far people are prevented from doing the things which matter. If negative or psychological freedom is emphasized, the fact that people have a limited number of opportunities would not mean of itself that they were not free, but their freedom is likely to be limited. If the stress falls on positive freedom, then the very fact that choices are limited means that freedom is limited. This point is easier to follow with a practical example. Mary is a frail elderly woman whose health is failing and who is finding it more and more difficult to cope. She has begun to have difficulty in remembering things; she sometimes leaves the cooker on, for example, after she has finished preparing a meal, which is a fire risk. Mary has the opportunity to move into a small flat supervised by a warden. She does not really want to move there, but she has little choice, and she is being pressed by various people – her relatives, her doctor, a social worker. She will be visited by a succession of people who can help with specific problems, doing the housework she cannot do, offering meals, or giving necessary personal care, like cutting her toe-nails. The effect this is considered to have on her personal freedom depends on the view that is taken. From the point of view of negative freedom, it seems to be a regrettable but necessary limitation of personal liberty in order to increase welfare. The idea of 'psychological' freedom suggests that the problem is misstated; Mary is already not free because she has lost the capacity to control her own life, and the details are less important than her failing mental faculties. 'Positive' freedom, by contrast, suggests that her freedom will be increased by moving into the flat with strong support from the social services, because this will increase her power to act in the future.

The distinction between the different kinds of freedom is sometimes useful, because the writers who consider freedom tend to stress one aspect or the other. However, it is also misleading in certain respects, because the elements of freedom cannot easily be separated from each other. MacCallum (1967) argues that all freedom is necessarily composed of the freedom *of* a person *from* restraints *to* do something – which means that all three concepts of freedom are involved to some degree. Negative freedom does, in practice, have to take into account a person's power to act and ability to choose; a person cannot be prevented from doing something he is unable to do. Equally, a person who is prevented from doing something does

not have the power to do it, which implies a restriction of positive
freedom as well. And the assumption that a person is competent to
exercise freedom, or able to become competent, is central both to
negative and positive concepts; without it, the ideas are meaningless.
In practice, advocates of any of these concepts of freedom have to
accept the others to some degree. Milton Friedman, for example,
writes of freedom as the 'absence of coercion' (Friedman 1962: 15),
but he also writes of people being 'free to choose' (Friedman 1981).
Berlin writes:

> It is argued, very plausibly, that if a man is too poor to afford
> something on which there is no legal ban – a loaf of bread, a
> journey round the world, resource to the law courts – he is as little
> free to have it as he would be if it were forbidden him by law. . . . If
> my poverty were a kind of disease, which prevented me from
> buying bread . . . as lameness prevents me from running, this
> inability would not naturally be described as a lack of freedom
> (Berlin 1969: 122)

Equally, though, one cannot write of people in poverty as being 'free
to choose' – it is the nature of poverty that people lack the power to
choose many things – and if 'freedom' is to have any force as a value,
the ability to choose has to be taken into account.

INDIVIDUAL AND SOCIAL CONCEPTS OF FREEDOM

The distinction between positive, negative, and psychological freedom is difficult to sustain in practice, and after it has been taken into
account, there are still important differences in the positions which
people take, which need to be explained. In many ways, the debate
on freedom reflects differing views not simply about the importance
of choice but also about the individual in society. There are both
individual and social models of freedom (see Spicker 1985). *Individual freedom* starts from the premise that each person determines
his or her own circumstances. The basic criterion is *autonomy*.
Individuals are free if they make their own decisions, subject only to
their own capabilities. Though the emphasis is likely to fall on
protection from coercion, the concept takes into account negative,

positive, and psychological freedom. It assumes that a person is not restricted, able to act, and able to make decisions. A person who is poor, disabled, or homeless is self-determining, and so is free.

The stress in the idea of individual welfare on the importance of what people want is strongly linked with the idea of individual freedom, the view, as expressed by J.S. Mill that 'Over himself, over his own body and mind, the individual is sovereign' (Mill 1859: 135). Intervention in individuals' lives, for their benefit or even to increase their freedom, is not legitimate without their consent, because it would be an interference with autonomy. The classic statement of this view is made by Mill, in his essay 'On Liberty':

> The object of this Essay is to assert one very simple principle. . . . That the only purpose for which power can rightfully be exercised over any member of a civilised community, against his will, is to prevent harm to others. His own good, either physical or moral, is not a sufficient warrant. . . . The only part of the conduct of any one, for which he is amenable to society, is that which concerns others. In the part which merely concerns himself, his independence is, of right, absolute.
>
> (*ibid.*)

There are many cases in which one person may 'harm' another, in which it would not necessarily be thought legitimate to prevent him. As Lucas points out:

> If I compete successfully for a scholarship or prize, I am in all probability doing somebody else out of it; if I buy my groceries from one shop rather than from its rival, I am depriving its rival of the profits it would otherwise have made.
>
> (Lucas 1966: 174)

This is certainly not what Mill intended. His primary concern is not really 'harm' to others as such, but interference with their autonomy – that is, their ability to act without being directly prevented from doing so by others. The central principle is one where the value of the freedom of each individual is paramount.

It is because autonomy is considered to be more important than welfare that intervention cannot be justified for an individual's own good. Although the point is contentious, it may be possible to reconcile intervention with individual freedom if the effect of the intervention is to make people more autonomous. The compulsory treatment of mentally ill people who are a 'danger' to themselves is an illustration. It is justifiable if it gives the person the power to make rational choices. It ceases to be justifiable when it limits autonomy – leading to the hazy but important distinction between 'psychiatric treatment in institutions' and 'institutionalization'.

The *social* model of freedom, by contrast, sees freedom primarily as a relationship between people. A person's capabilities, powers, and choices are not formed in isolation; they depend on the structure of the society of which he is a part. 'Basic' freedoms, like freedom of assembly, political participation, and economic freedom have to be understood in a social context. 'Freedom', Tawney argues, 'is always relative to power' (Tawney 1931: 107). Where the individual model emphasizes self-determination, the social model stresses the power to act; where the individual model refers to freedom from coercion, the social model is concerned with the maximization of people's opportunities – which may mean restricting the actions of others. The social model justifies intervention in people's lives to liberate them from restricted circumstances. In the same way that individual freedom can be linked with the idea of individual welfare, the social concept of freedom has to be considered in the light of the discussion of social welfare. Both freedom and welfare are defined in social terms; both are relative to the position of others. As with welfare, there may be conflicts of interest. Freedom can be increased by increasing power. Money is one source of power: because money makes choice possible, a person with more money is more free. Equally, because power is relative, a person's freedom may be increased by reducing the power of others. Barry argues against this view that 'to enslave someone is not normally said to increase the slave-owner's freedom, though it certainly decreases the slave's' (quoted in Plant, Lesser, and Taylor-Gooby 1980: 195). Taylor-Gooby replies that 'It is perfectly sensible to describe slave ownership as enhancing the master's freedom so long as it enables him to do things that he wants to do' (*ibid.*: 196). By the social concept, therefore, the provision of welfare increases the freedom of some at the expense of others.

In both these models of freedom, freedom is inextricably bound up with welfare. The individual concept is linked with the view that the best judge of interests are likely to be the people involved; the social concept interprets welfare in large part as dependent on the power to achieve well-being, though it also sees the satisfaction of needs as essential to freedom. Freedom is essential to serve a person's basic interests.

SELF-DETERMINATION IN SOCIAL WORK

An illustration of the place of these concepts in welfare provision is the idea of *self-determination* in social work. Social work developed in large part from the Christian beliefs of nineteenth-century reformers, and social work still shares with Christianity a stress on individual freedom, subject to moral constraints. People can only act morally if they are responsible for their actions; and they cannot be responsible for their actions if they are not free to choose. Freedom is important, then, not simply as an end in itself but as a means to moral action. Some writers refer to a concept of *moral* freedom, which is the power to act morally. The idea implies 'self-mastery', but in order to be truly free a person must also make the right decisions.

'Self-determination' is a central feature of the social worker's Code of Ethics; it is for each client to decide for himself/herself whether to accept the advice and guidance of a social worker. However, the idea of 'self-determination' is, as Bernstein argues, very unclear (Bernstein 1975). It could mean acceptance of what the person expresses as a want. It could mean what a person 'really' wants, when non-verbal cues and uncertainty have been taken into account. 'Self-determination' may mean self-determinaton within 'realistic' limits. It may be subject to the needs and rights of others; the degree of 'self-determination' which probation officers encourage in a client does not generally extend to criminal activity. It could mean 'rational' self-determination – a term which is liable to abuse, for a person may be considered 'rational' when they do the sorts of things that they are supposed to do, like paying gas bills, and 'irrational' when they do not. And it may mean, lastly, building a person's self-respect and personality – fostering autonomy and moral freedom, rather than observing a principle of non-interference. (This is the view taken, for example, by Perlman 1975).

The principle of self-determination is closely linked with an individual concept of freedom. J.S. Mill wrote that the individual

> cannot rightfully be compelled to do or forbear because it will be better for him to do so, because it will make him happier, because, in the opinion of others, to do so would be wise, or even right. These may be good reasons for remonstrating with him, or reasoning with him, or persuading him, or entreating him, but not for compelling him, or visiting him with any evil in case he do otherwise. To justify that, the conduct from which it is desired to deter him must be calculated to produce evil to some one else.
>
> (Mill 1859: 135)

But even this may be too large a concession; the very fact of having a social worker beating a path to one's door may be taken as an infringement of personal freedom. The principle of self-determination seems to imply that one should not interfere in other people's lives. In one social-work method, 'non-directive coun-selling', it is considered inappropriate for the social worker to offer any advice at all; the function of the counsellor is to help individuals come to terms with their feelings, recognize and express personal desires, and to formulate their own plans of action.

The principle of 'self-determination' means, Soyer argues, that social work clients have a 'right to fail' (Soyer 1975). Clients are entitled to make their own decisions, to take their own risks, without interference by the social worker. This is based on two important criteria. In the first place, the client may be right, and the social worker wrong; the idea that the social worker knows better is an assumption one cannot legitimately make. Clients are likely, for example, to have a better idea of what they want, what they feel, and what they are capable of than a social worker does. The rejoin-der to this is that social workers often *do* know better – as, in other contexts, do doctors, health visitors, or teachers. In part this repre-sents specialized knowledge, and experience of similar situations; in part, their relative emotional detachment; and, perhaps most im-portant, the application of social values – because, even if the indi-vidual is right, this may be at the expense of others. If the person's 'right to fail' means, for example, long-term dependency on welfare benefits, it is at least arguable whether the person can have free choice at the expense of others. The second criterion is that people need to make their own decisions in order to develop moral freedom; it is the process by which they learn to use and to value freedom. This is a strong argument; the main objection to it is that 'the right to fail' must also, to be worthwhile, encompass a power to succeed. There are more constructive ways of helping someone at the bottom of a deep pit than to tell him he is perfectly free to try to climb out.

The concept of self-determination rests in a concept of individual freedom which sees the individual as a rational, autonomous actor. The social concept of freedom offers a different approach. People's abilities are formed in a social context, and it is uncertain whether they can be seen as fully autonomous individuals. Poverty or stress may incapacitate a person. But the reasons for the problem often lie outside the individual, and it is unrealistic to treat someone as fully self-determining who is a victim of circumstances. Wilding and George attack the individualist approach as unsociological – that is, ignoring the social realities – and restrictive of freedom, because in refusing to recognize these limitations it also denies the steps necessary to deal with them (Wilding and George 1975). This position is reflected in social work to varying degrees. *Systems theory* is an attempt to see individuals in the context of their social environment; the social worker's task is to identify key influences and settings through which it may be possible to bring about change. *Radical social work* (see Bailey and Brake 1975) rejects the individualistic approach altogether; social workers must, its advocates argue, seek to promote changes in the structure of society. Because the problems do not stem from the individual, any solution which seeks to deal with problems on an individual basis are doomed to failure.

The principle of self-determination certainly has to be greatly modified if it is to apply to social-work practice at all. Much of the theory has been formed from a concern with the emotional problems of adults. Social work in Britain is substantially constrained by the legal responsibilities passed to Social Services Departments. The principal client groups are children at risk of abuse or neglect, offenders, old people, physically disabled people, mentally handicapped people, and mentally ill people. Unless the case occurs in one of a few specifically defined settings, or affects an existing client, social workers are not responsible for problems like emotional distress or divorce; it can be difficult within institutional constraints to do any work in areas like drug abuse or suicide. These problems tend in many local authorities to be tackled as opportunities arise – a medical social worker may learn about an attempted suicide in hospital, and if fortunate will have a day or two before the patient is discharged – or left to the voluntary sector. In other work done by social workers, most obviously in probation, the role of the worker may include a degree of control over the client's actions. And although most social workers working with children at risk would see the family, not just the child, as their client, and spend much time with the adults, there is clearly a limit to the degree of independence which can be afforded to parents who are likely to abuse or neglect the child. The effect of this limitation of responsibilities is to reduce the power of social workers to apply the principles emphasized in their training, and the application of different methods and principles, including how far a client is allowed 'self-determination', tends to be piecemeal and inconsistent.

PATERNALISM

If one considers welfare to be morally right, then it seems to be right, on the face of the matter, to do something which benefits people as long as it does not harm others. However, Mill's arguments on individual freedom – which are echoed, for example, by Robert Nozick (1974) – imply that people should be able to choose not to receive welfare; more than this, they are free actually to do harm to themselves if they please. The position seems extreme. Welfare is, at least in part, linked to what people want, and the principle of consent in welfare is widely accepted as important. Social security must be claimed to be received. People who disapprove of certain forms of medical care – like Christian Scientists – can refuse treatment. Health care is compulsory only when the individual is deemed to be incapable of withholding consent, and recently the power of mental patients to refuse treatment has been established by the 1983 Mental Health Act. Equally, though, there are examples of welfare provision in which the consent of the people who benefit has not been asked, or

Table 4.1 *Forms of paternalism*

	'Pure'	'Impure'
'Legal' (prevention of harm)	Seat-belt legislation	Alcohol licensing
'Extreme' (positive benefit)	State pensions	Statutory sick pay (employers are required to pay sick employees)

even (in cases like the provision of a water supply or legislation to remove unfit housing) in which there is an element of compulsion. The principle of doing things for people without their consent is known as *paternalism*. Marshall writes, 'it would be dishonest to pretend that there is not about welfare policy decisions something intrinsically authoritarian or . . . paternalistic' (Marshall 1981: 109). 'Paternalism' is a pejorative word, but it represents a strongly felt set of moral beliefs. To take a simple example, imagine that you have dropped in unexpectedly on a friend. There is no answer at the door, but it is unlocked, and you go in. You find your friend lying on the settee. On the table there is an empty bottle of pills, and a note which says 'I want to die. Please leave me alone.' What would you do? If you do *not* leave it there, you are acting paternalistically. If your intervention is justified, it is because your concern for your friend's welfare is more important than your friend's freedom to choose – or, to be more precise, your friend's negative freedom. From the viewpoint of positive freedom, I think the argument can be made that suicide denies freedom, because it denies any further power to choose; it is not, therefore, an option that can legitimately be chosen.

In policy terms, paternalism implies rules which restrict people for their own benefit. Dworkin distinguishes *pure paternalism* and *impure paternalism* (Dworkin 1979). Pure paternalism includes those measures which directly benefit the person who is restricted: an example is fluoridization of the water supply. Impure paternalism is where another person is restricted to prevent people from harming themselves, like restrictions on gambling establishments. Feinberg further distinguishes paternalism which prevents harm to oneself, which he calls *legal paternalism*, from paternalism which actually benefits the individual, which is *extreme paternalism* (Feinberg 1973). These categories, together with Dworkin's classification, help to outline some of the dimensions of paternalism. Table 4.1 gives examples of each.

The justifications for paternalistic policies are outlined by Dworkin (1981). There is the argument that people need to have policies made on their behalf because of ignorance about the possible consequences. So, for example, policies to protect people from the spread of disease are implemented because experts 'know better'. There is the view that people have weak wills and behave unreasonably, even though they know they shouldn't, unless someone tells them what to do – like wearing crash helmets on motorcycles – or does it for them – like providing state insurance or medical care. This extends into the payment of benefits in kind because people are likely to spend cash unwisely – like food stamps in the United States, or clothing vouchers in Britain; it is worth pointing out that any provision of goods which might be paid for in the private market, like food, education, and housing, might be thought of as 'paternalistic' (the case is made by Seldon 1977). There is also the case that people may by ill-placed to make their own decisions – the person who attempts suicide is probably suffering from emotional stress which impairs their judgement. In the extreme form, this view is taken when people have diminished rationality – for example, through mental illness or mental handicap – and are deemed to be incapable of making decisions for themselves.

A number of further justifications can be added to Dworkin's list of reasons. One is that people should not have to be bothered with making certain decisions. A person who is well-paid can go to an accountant for advice about financial affairs; a poor person goes to a welfare-rights centre. The person with the accountant will have everything taken care of. The welfare-rights centre will probably encourage people to help themselves, in the best tradition of self-determination – which means the clients have to do much of the work. It may be 'paternalistic' to remove anxieties from people's lives, but that is not of itself undesirable. The main reservation must be that the client retains ultimate control – which is not at all the same thing as having to make the decisions. In other words, paternalism should be, as Weale argues, consistent with a person's wants (Weale 1978).

Paternalism can be seen as a social system – a system some critics call the 'nanny state', as if there was something wrong with the state protecting people. On the front cover of Seldon's book *Charge!* are the questions:

> If you had a choice in spending your money, would you waste it unnecessarily when your children needed schooling and your wife needed a doctor?
>   If not, what makes you think other people would?
>   If they wouldn't, why don't we give money to people who need it and leave everyone free in spending it?
>
> (Seldon 1977)

The reasons why other people might spend their money on other things – and that I might – is that rational people take risks; they gamble against uncertainty, measuring a certain present cost against an uncertain future benefit. That does not mean that risks are desirable; it only means that they are there. The risk may seem too slight to guard against; the cost of insurance may seem unfair to a person whose risks are lower than other people's. But what is uncertain for an individual is within a social context much more certain: some people will be disabled, some poor, some homeless, even if we do not know precisely who they will be at the outset. The freedom to spend money as one chooses is only superficially desirable; it creates options to become impoverished through sickness and old age. Part of the purpose of welfare is to reduce the need to take these risks within a society as a whole. Some limitation of this 'freedom' – a degree of paternalism – is essential to the good life.

Third, paternalism may increase freedom. Freedom is not only negative freedom, the absence of interference; it includes positive and psychological concepts. Paternalism may increase a person's power to choose, either by establishing the material foundations which are necessary for autonomy in society or by developing a person's ability to choose through education. It ceases to be justifiable on this ground when it limits freedom – leading to the distinction between education and indoctrination.

Lastly, paternalism may be the moral thing to do. If welfare is right, it does not necessarily cease to be right just because the recipient objects to it. When a person chooses to do something which is destructive of welfare – like attempting suicide or refusing medical treatment – there may be a tendency to accuse the person of diminished rationality as an excuse to do the moral thing anyway. In such a case the importance of welfare has to be balanced against individual choice, and it is only if individual choice is seen as 'supreme' that welfare will never outweigh it.

V

Rights

Summary: *Rights are rules which protect liberties or impose duties on other people. One view of rights is that people have them when they stand to benefit from the obligations others have towards them; another is that they can legitimately choose what other people will do. Rights may be particular to some people, or general, applying to everyone. Like morals, they are socially defined in practice, and even 'human' rights, which seem at first to apply to everyone, are interpreted differently for children, for example, than for adults.*

'Citizenship' is a basis for a person's rights in a society. Rights are 'positive' when they are enforceable, and much of the value of rights is that they require people to behave in certain ways in order to increase social welfare.

Rights, like morals, are rules which govern social relationships. When a person has a right, it affects the way that other people ought to behave. Many rights correspond directly to duties, and Benn and Peters argue that, in general, if I have a duty towards you, then you have a right against me (Benn and Peters 1959, Ch. 4). But not all rights can conveniently be described like this. The 'right' to speak one's mind, for example, implies no clear obligation on other people – they don't have to stand there and listen. And although I may recognize a moral obligation or duty to give charity, this does not necessarily mean that everyone has a right against me if I fail to give it.

Hohfield refers to four different kinds of rights: claim rights, liberties, powers, and immunities ([1923], quoted in Weale 1983, Ch. 7). *Claim-rights* are rights which imply duties on other people. An example might be claims for social-security benefits; decisions can be appealed against if the right is not administered properly. *Liberties* do not imply clear duties, but they might prevent certain types of action by other people – like the right of 'free speech', or the right to refuse social workers entry to one's home. *Powers* make it possible for people to do things which others cannot. A driving licence is a simple example; the idea can be extended, straightforwardly enough, to other types of licence, like the licence to run a private nursing home. It might also be argued to include the rights of parents over children. Lastly, *immunities* exempt a person from duties which apply to other people. Disabled people are immune from parking restrictions which apply to others. Tax relief is arguably another immunity – though it can also be seen as a claim-right. It is not always clear which of these categories a right falls into; what, for example, is 'the right to work'?

The scope of rights, the extent to which powers are conferred by them and duties imposed, are often uncertain. There are two common ways of describing the way rights work. Hart argues, I think correctly, that freedom is the most basic kind of right (Hart 1955). Liberties, powers, and immunities are all forms of negative liberty – they emphasize non-interference; claim-rights, too, depend on a form of negative liberty, because they assume logically that the person who is obliged to meet the claim is free to do things unless a claim exists. Equally, different rights may be a means to assert positive freedom. The central case for claim-rights is that though they limit the freedom of some, they increase the power to act of others. This emphasis on freedom prompts the idea that people must be able to use and control their rights. This is at the heart of the first view, the *will* or *power theory*. A person has a right against another when he can legitimately choose to alter the way in which another person should act. On the face of it, this might suggest that children do not have rights against social workers, because they are not considered able to choose. This does not mean, though, that a child could not have a legitimate claim. Hart argues that 'A right entails having a moral justification for limiting the freedom of another person and for determining how he should act' (Hart 1955: 183). The test here is not that a person does choose, or even that a person could choose; a mentally and physically handicapped person who is unable to object to the way he is treated would still legitimately be entitled to object. The test is one of moral justification – *should* a person have a choice? On this basis, it may well be that children in these circumstances could still be said to have a right.

The main objection to the will theory is that there are cases in which we do talk about 'rights' but have no choice in the matter – notably the 'right' to education. If a child has a right to be educated, and this implies choice, can there be a duty to attend school? One possible answer to this objection is that there is no duty on the child to attend school; the duty, in Britain at least, falls on the parents; but this does not deal with the point, because the child is still under compulsion and has no claim to any choice in the matter. We can argue that education is a prerequisite for other rights – without it, a child would be deprived of other choices later – but it would be odd, on the terms of the will theory, to talk about education as a right in itself.

The second view is called the *benefit theory*, or *interest theory*. According to this theory, a person has a right when another person has an obligation towards him from which he stands to benefit. By this argument, children have a right to be protected from their parents by local authority social workers, because social workers have a duty to protect them. A similar argument is made by Campbell (1983). He argues that rights are based on interests: a right is an interest protected by rules. The objection to the benefit theory is a logical one. One person may oblige another to help a third: A requires B to help C. B's duty is not to C, the beneficiary, but to A. This is found in practice in the operation of charitable trusts. The trustees may have a duty to help 'the poor', but no specific poor person has a right to receive this help. (This argument extends to the issues of Chapter 3; the moral obligations of altruism are not sufficient to create social rights. If rights are to be gained, others have to recognize a direct obligation; there may be, then, a sense in which rights may have to be 'earned' through some form of reciprocity.)

Neither of these theories is, then, wholly satisfactory. It may be that the truth lies in some sort of compromise between the different theories; it may also be that the theories are unsatisfactory because the idea of 'rights' compounds a number of different concepts. The appeal of the benefit theory is that it helps to establish a basis for claiming welfare as a right; the will theory stresses the importance of deciding for oneself. They both have, then, a distinct moral basis, which is as important to their advocates as their analytical power.

THE BASIS OF RIGHTS

The claim to a 'right' is a strong one. Rights fall, in general, into two main classes: *moral rights* and *positive rights*. A person holds a moral right when he or she has a moral claim or justification to a course of action. A positive right is one which is legally enforceable. Positive rights may also be moral rights, but there are positive rights which have a very uncertain moral basis – it is possible to take a complaint against a general practitioner for the behaviour of a relief doctor – and moral rights which have no effective means of enforcement, like the 'right to work'.

Moral rights may be *particular* or *general*. Particular rights are specific to an individual – like the right of an individual to have a promise kept. General rights apply to everyone, or at least everyone in a category (like 'children', 'parents', or 'mentally ill people'). These general rights can be seen as *natural* or *social*. Natural rights are said to be moral rights of individuals which exist by virtue of their natures. Natural rights which apply to everyone are sometimes referred to as 'human rights'; everyone has them by virtue of being human. They include, for example, the rights to 'life, liberty, and the pursuit of happiness' assumed in the US Declaration of Independence. The Universal Declaration of Human Rights agreed by the United Nations extends this to cover 'the economic, social and cultural rights indispensable for [the individual's] dignity and the free development of his personality' (Article 22), and 'a standard of living adequate for health and well-being of himself and his family, including food, clothing, housing and medical care and necessary social services' (Article 25(1)).

Cranston believes that the scope of human rights cannot legitimately be extended in this manner. A right can only be a 'human' right if it is *practicable* (Cranston 1976). A person cannot have a right to what is impossible, and 'medical care', for example, can only be provided under certain contingencies, depending on both the nature of the illness and on the technical capacity of medical practitioners. There could be no right to hip replacement before hip replacements became possible. A human right must be applicable to all people in all circumstances, or *universal*. The right to 'holidays with pay' cannot be a human right, because not everyone is employed. And a human right must be of *paramount importance*, and Cranston does not think that social and economic rights are.

Watson criticizes Cranston's criteria as too stringent (Watson 1977). The test of 'practicability' is too wide; it should, rather, be a general requirement to do what we can. The provision of welfare *is*, he writes, of paramount importance – a view I share, for a right to life is vitiated without the conditions, like food and shelter, that help to make life livable. And 'universality' is too restrictive; many rights, like the right to a 'fair trial', depend on the circumstances specific to a particular society, and rights to social security or employment are affected by similar considerations.

Cranston's insistence on 'universality' seems to suggest that he sees human rights as natural, an intrinsic part of the human condition. If we see rights as a system of social rules, an individual cannot have rights outside society. It is only if rights are seen as something inherent in the individual – a position taken by Locke (1690), and by Nozick (1974) – that they can exist divorced from a social context. Rights which belong to everyone in a particular situation – like rights to support in old age, to a minimum income, or to health care – may be 'natural', but it makes more sense to see them as socially determined, because they depend on a set of social circumstances. This does not mean that rights to welfare cannot be human rights, but rather that human rights are themselves social in form; we are social animals.

CHILDREN'S RIGHTS

The issue of rights for children raises a number of special issues. Freeman identifies four main classes of rights of children (Freeman 1983). In the first place, there are the rights that an adult may also have – like rights to life, liberty, or the pursuit of happiness. But the rights of children are not often equivalent to those of adults. They are not entitled to vote, to work, to leave home, to marry, or have sexual relationships. Their choices and opportunities are substantially limited.

Second, children have rights to welfare. In some ways these rights are like those of adults; they include rights to food, shelter, health care, and the basic essentials of life. Necessarily, these rights have to be interpreted in the light of the circumstances of children, who are in general likely to be dependent on adults. In practice, however, this is often taken to suggest that the rights of children are rights of a different kind. The UN Declaration of the Rights of the Child (1959) defines the children's rights explicitly in terms differently to adults:

> The child, for the full and harmonious development of his personality, needs love and understanding. He shall, wherever possible, grow up in the care and under the responsibility of his parents, and in any case in an atmosphere of affection and of moral and material security.
>
> (UN Declaration 1959, Principle 6)

There is no mention, in the UN Universal Declaration of Human Rights, of the rights of adults to affection, love, understanding, or moral security – which is not to say that their need is less.

The distinction made between the rights of children and adults reflects, clearly, commonly accepted social differences in their status. But if both kinds of rights are 'human', it effectively means there are different categories of human being. There are reasons why children and adults should, as a general proposition, be treated differently. Freeman's third category concerns 'protective' rights. The child is treated as specially vulnerable 'by reason of his physical and mental immaturity' (in the Preamble to the UN Declaration). This is a paternalistic argument. Freeman gives a striking case for paternalism in the case of Ricky Green from Pennsylvania, a 16-year-old child with a curved spine who required an operation to prevent him from becoming permanently bedridden (Freeman 1983: 256–7). His mother, a Jehovah's witness, refused consent to the blood transfusions necessary for the operation. The court consulted the boy's opinion; he agreed with his mother, and the court decided the operation should not proceed. Freeman argues that the child was being denied the opportunity for what a dissenting judge called 'any semblance of a normal life'. The child was not able to exercise an independent judgement, and his decision would prevent him from ever being able to do so. The case for intervention – 'liberal paternalism' – is that it would increase the child's freedom.

This is, clearly, a contentious position, because it implies restrictions on both parent and child. But the principles it raises can be extended well beyond the scope of children; there are adults who are vulnerable and immature, and adults are also subject to 'neglect, cruelty, and exploitation' (Principle 9). The same case can almost certainly be applied to people who are mentally ill or mentally handicapped. It probably applies to many old people, and it could arguably be extended to cover those issues, like decisions about health care, which people are often not competent to judge and leave to specialists.

Harris argues that there are no arguments for the differential treatment of children which cannot be extended to adults, and that children should be treated as equal to adults. This does not mean that they should be treated the same, but as having the same rights:

> If children are regarded as the equals of adults, then they are entitled to equal protection, as being entitled to be shown the same concern and respect as adults. . . . To regard people as equals is to take a stand on how they are to be treated, not to make a remark about their capabilities.

(Harris 1982: 49)

There are cases in which one can say the rights of children have been infringed, on the same basis that the rights of adults would be. Freeman gives the example of the use of drugs to control the behaviour of children in residential care (Freeman 1983: 172–3). But in many cases it is not possible to generalize about the position of children from the rights of adults, and it is difficult to apply Harris's argument to the circumstances in which children are actually brought up. Freeman's fourth, and final, category concerns rights against parents. Special rules have to be made because of the nature of the relationship between parents and children. If children have exactly the same rights as adults, it is difficult to see how a parent could morally put to bed a tired but unwilling infant, or change the nappy of a toddler who has something more interesting to do. I am doubtful that either of these actions can be seen as increasing the child's autonomy – though putting the child to bed might increase the parent's.

Parents, it can be argued, have rights too. These rights are not absolute, because they are determined by the rights of the child. In a recent historic judgment, the House of Lords decided that parental rights 'exist for the benefit of the child and they are justified only in so far as they enable the parent to perform his duties towards the child' (Fraser LJ, quoted in the *Guardian*, 18 October 1985, p. 4). This provides a justification for limiting parental rights in certain cases – for example, intervention in the family in the event of the abuse or neglect of children. But there are many more reasons for intervention. Local authorities may seek to remove a child from a family because it is in 'moral danger', or because it is beyond the control of the parents. And under the 1980 Child Care Act, the authorities may assume parental rights – removing the rights from the natural parent – when the parent is unable to look after the child, has failed to do so, or is deemed to be unfit because of unsuitable habits or 'mode of life'. Law is not always representative of morality, but this helps to illustrate the limitations of 'parental rights'; the interests of the child are treated as prior to the interests of the parents. But rights depend on a social context, and in the case of children this demands some recognition of the role of the family.

RIGHTS AND CITIZENSHIP

Rights are held by individuals as citizens. Citizenship has been described by Judge Earl Warren as 'a man's basic right, for it is nothing less than the right to have rights' (quoted in Goodin 1982: 77). Citizenship is a formal recognition of the claims and responsibilities of individuals as members of a society. Marshall describes citizenship as 'a status bestowed on those who are full members of a community. All those who possess the status are equal with respect to the rights and duties with which the status is endowed' (Marshall 1963: 87). Marshall assumes that these rights and duties apply equally to all. But the concept of citizenship does not necessarily apply to everyone; it may exclude people as well as including them. It may cover only certain categories of people, like adults, males, or whites. In Israel, some Arabs are citizens, and entitled to all social services; some (e.g. in Jerusalem) are 'residents', not citizens, but still receive services; and others, in the occupied or 'administered' territory of Gaza and the West Bank, have been treated since 1967 as citizens of other countries who are not entitled to a full range of services.

Citizenship can be contingent on certain criteria; in the days of the Poor Law, people who were dependent on relief ceased to have the rights of citizens (like the right to vote or to take legal action). It may depend on 'civic competence' – a provision which has led to the denial, in the past, of rights for women, mentally handicapped people, and blacks in the United States (before literacy tests were declared unconstitutional). It is still true that mentally ill people who are committed for treatment in the United Kingdom cease to have important rights – like the right to vote – which are allowed to others; it is only recently that the right to vote has been upheld for mentally handicapped people in institutions.

The case for denying people rights according to competence is twofold. One is linked with the 'will' theory of rights; if rights rely on choice, then, as Goodin points out, people who are unable to exercise choice are unable to be citizens (Goodin 1982: 78). The second argument, made by Ackerman, is closely related; it is that a person must be able to enter into a dialogue with others in order to make a political society possible. Citizenship, as a status, implies participation in this dialogue; it is meaningless for those who cannot participate. On this basis, he believes mentally handicapped people should not be citizens (Ackerman 1980: 79–80).

This position is, I think, misconceived. In the first place, even if actual competence is an appropriate requirement, the competence of people who are mentally handicapped should not be underestimated. Nirje details requests made by mentally retarded delegates to a conference in Stockholm – requests which are clear, unequivocal, and eminently reasonable. For example, they state:

> We want to choose our own furniture, and have our own furniture in the room. . . .
> When we are living in institutions, we want social training so as to be able to move out into society and manage on our own. . . .
> We want . . . to have our own key when we live at home. . . .
> We do not want to be used on our jobs by being given the worst and most boring tasks. . . .
> We demand to have more information about our handicap.
>   (quoted in Nirje 1972: 189–93)

Second, the exclusion of people may have the effect of making them incompetent – the argument against women's suffrage in the nineteenth century, or black power in South Africa – when they are quite capable of developing competence. Third, there is Harris's view that rights determine how people are treated, not on their capabilities. The criterion of competence imposes a condition on rights which is based on practical ability rather than moral force. (All of these arguments apply to some degree to children; the limitations on their rights are made for other, social, reasons.)

People who are entitled to do something should not be less entitled because they are unable to exercise their right. An elderly woman who is isolated and housebound through failing health should not lose her rights because she is unable to exercise them effectively. A person who has rights has them *as if* he or she was competent to use them; incompetence does not refute the right but creates a distinct moral problem – how to enforce the principle.

WELFARE RIGHTS

Positive rights are rights which have a sanction, or means of enforcement. To put it another way, if I can legitimately make someone do something, then I have a right against that person.

In some opinions, this means that the question of enforcement is rather more important than the principle behind it. One interpretation of rights is that they consist of 'claims', pressed on various grounds, whether moral or legal. This is the position taken by Rein (1983, Ch. 2). The argument is not that rights do not convey a moral obligation, but that it does not matter very much if they do or don't; the point of interest is whether rights actually regulate relationships, not whether they are morally justifiable. To explain behaviour, it is necessary only to examine how claims are made, how strongly they are pressed, what sanctions are applied. The concept of 'rights', in other words, is redundant.

The value of this argument is that, when certain kinds of 'right' are claimed – the 'right to work', for example, or 'parental rights' – it is possible to reply that 'these concepts have no intrinsic interest; the only point that is worth examining is how the claims are backed up'. It offers a different way of looking at the problems. But it tends to underestimate the moral force of certain rights. There is no obvious reason why we should pay any attention to some 'claims', like the right of children neglected by parents, or of wives beaten by husbands, except for our moral principles, because both groups in practice are relatively powerless otherwise. It is possible to reply to this, cynically, that very little attention has been paid to these issues in the past – for a long time, many doctors refused to accept that parents might abuse their children, and the problems of battered wives have not exactly been dealt with energetically by public or social services. This does not invalidate the point, though, because certain issues – like child abuse or the ill-treatment of mentally handicapped people in institutions – have become the focus of strong moral feeling; the claim is based in moral opinion, and it is not possible to explain the strength of the claim without considering the moral case.

The movement, in the United Kingdom and the United States, for 'welfare rights' has been in part an attempt to convert moral rights into positive ones, but it has also used existing positive rights, in the legal system, to establish a moral position. The welfare rights movement – if a number of different kinds of organization, with mixed aims and methods, working in similar fields can be called a 'movement' – has tried in a number of ways to establish a right to a basic minimum income. Legal remedies have been used to challenge decisions made about individual cases, with the intention of making practice conform to stated rules. Cases of this sort have a dual purpose. The aim is not only to protect the position of those who are vulnerable but also to establish the general principle of rights to welfare. This can be seen as a justification of the activity even if the individuals in question are not ultimately successful.

Welfare rights have been used to challenge – with mixed success – the legitimacy of existing rules. Special financial needs, for the poorest claimants in the United Kingom, were met until 1980 at the discretion of the Supplementary Benefits Commission. The use of this discretion was challenged with increasing frequency during the 1970s, and a review of Supplementary Benefit concluded that payments should be made by legal regulation – enforceable rights – rather than by discretion. Although the government attempted severely to retrench, by refusing to allow most payments for clothing, the effect of this change was massively to increase the number of

claims made successfully and the cost of the scheme as a whole. (The
government has now abolished these rights and introduced a
discretionary system with strict cash limits and no right of appeal – a
proposal which has already attracted, from CPAG, the promise of
litigation.)

Where legal remedies seemed likely to be ineffective, protest has
taken other forms – like the occupation of social-security waiting-
rooms by claimants' groups. This type of activity has been done in the
United Kingdom by the Claimants' Unions, organizations which
have sometimes achieved gains for certain claimants (see Jordan
1973) but whose parochial basis and preference for confrontation
has tended to limit their contribution to the wider debate.

Lastly, arguments about rights have been used as a means to
establish principles. In 1969 Tony Lynes wrote, 'the fact is that *nobody* –
except a few cranks in the Child Poverty Action Group – really thinks
of Supplementary Benefit as a right' (Lynes 1969: 5). It is impossible to
say exactly how far there has been a shift in opinion, and if so, why it has
happened; but by 1984, 84 per cent of claimants thought that
Supplementary Benefit was, on the whole, a right (PSI 1984: A12a).

The concepts current in welfare rights work are trenchantly
criticized by Campbell, ostensibly from a socialist position (Campbell
1983, Ch. 10). He argues that the emphasis on the rights of a person
is highly destructive. It induces complacency about the effectiveness
of the system; increases the sense of dependency of claimants;
stigmatizes people who do not have rights, by contrast with those who
do; places a heavy burden on the legal system, which leads to
inefficiency; creates absurd problems and unfairness through the
complexity of the system (e.g. people being worse off in work than on
benefit); and it may have unforeseen side-effects (he gives the
example of maternity leave, which he thinks discourages employers
from taking on women).

I must confess here to a strong personal bias; I was first drawn into
welfare-rights work while at college, and have been actively involved
for at least ten of the last fourteen years. Perhaps unsurprisingly,
then, I disagree with Campbell's arguments. Welfare-rights work
does not induce complacency; on the contrary, it draws attention to
those areas in which the practice of welfare provision falls below the
standard that is generally claimed for it. It is far from clear that rights

increase dependency. In the health service, the establishment of rights for all seems to have reduced any sense of dependency, in contrast with other services which do not have these rights; a survey by Blaxter shows significantly different attitudes to free prescriptions from other types of means tested benefits, because one is 'health' and the other is not (Blaxter 1974). The examples Campbell gives of unfairness seem to stem from too few rights rather than too many. Rights to minimum wages while working would make sure that no-one is better off on the dole; paternity leave would mean employers having nothing to gain by preferring men because women have maternity leave. If people are stigmatized because they do not have rights which others have – a point which is arguable, because stigma is more deep-rooted than this suggests – the answer seems to be to extend the same rights to them, not to take them away from the others. An emphasis on the rights of everyone undermines the force of his objection. And Campbell has overlooked the campaigning aspects and political intentions behind welfare rights. The increasing legal burden and complex development of rules have been part of a strategy to change these rules.

It is far from clear that a strategy to increase rights can overcome the problems of stigma and social rejection described in Chapter 3. But positive rights are still important. They are a means of protection against the disadvantages which are suffered by people who are poor and dependent. They help to guarantee a minimum standard of material well-being. And they define the status of the recipient as a citizen – which matters, not only from the point of view of the individual but because the idea of welfare as a right of citizenship entails a general commitment to social provision.

PART 2

The Welfare State

VI

Social services and the welfare state

Summary: *Social services are social institutions developed to provide for those conditions of dependency which are recognized as collective responsibilities. The 'welfare state' is based on a recognition of dependency as a normal element of social relationships. In theory, the welfare state offers protection to all its citizens at the best possible level. In practice, though, 'welfare states' are defined historically, not by their closeness to an ideal. The state may provide services, in so far as state intervention is accepted as legitimate, but the role of the 'state' is complex; it also supervises the provision of welfare in the whole society, regulating, mandating, stimulating, and supporting alternative channels of welfare provision.*

THE NATURE OF A SOCIAL SERVICE

The idea of a 'social service' is conventionally used in a fairly narrow way. The main areas usually referred to are medical care, social security, housing, education, and social work. Titmuss argued in a seminal essay that this approach is too restrictive, and that it leads to inconsistencies in the way in which welfare is discussed (Titmuss 1955a). To take two contemporary examples of the sort of thing he was writing about, government subsidies to tenants are 'social services', but subsidies to owner-occupiers are not; job creation is a social service, but the regulation, subsidy, and economic control of industry to promote employment is not. The use of the terms seems fairly arbitrary.

Social services are distinguished less by what they do than the way in which they do it. In the first place, social services have to be organized activities. The provision of social welfare can be informal; much of the care provided by a family becomes a 'social service' when it is taken over by a welfare agency. A 'voluntary social service' is more than the work done by an individual volunteer, or a helpful neighbour; it means social welfare provision run by a voluntary organization.

Second, social services are redistributive; that is to say, the people who pay are not the same as the people who benefit. Many occupations and services involve activities which in a different context might be 'social services'; grocers, accountants, and hoteliers are possible examples. However, these type of services are not 'social', unlike some other schemes which might seem at first sight to be similar – like meals on wheels, welfare-rights advice, or residential homes for the elderly.

There are some organized activities which are social and redistributive but are not classified as 'social services'. They are usually referred to as 'public' services. They include the police, the army, roads, refuse collection, parks, and many others. They are collective services which benefit (in principle) the whole community. The same, of course, could be said for many social services. The health service and education offer universal coverage and are likely to be used by almost everyone at some time. The existence of a safety net in social security – 'from the cradle to the grave', in theory if not always in practice – is a reassurance to more people than will actually find themselves in financial difficulties. The distinction between public and social services may, then, be difficult to sustain. Public housing, for example, is thought of as a social service, and libraries are a public service. But both are publicly provided; both benefit the individuals who use them at the expense of others.

In part, the distinction is made because social services have a *residual* function – acting as a safety net when other methods fail. Eyden defines a social service as '*a social institution that has developed to meet the personal needs of individual members of society not adequately or effectively met by either the individual from his own or his family's resources or by commercial or industrial concerns*' (Eyden, quoted in Byrne and Padfield 1978: 1). This implies, first, that social services respond to the problems of individuals, and second, that they do so only when other methods have failed. In both respects, this seems too limited. Social services are not concerned only with individuals: they also provide for families, groups, and communities. And they may be provided, like the British health or education services, without regard to other resources that people may have.

However, the fact that social services are sometimes described in this way helps to explain the difference between social and public services. The distinction rests on the way we view the recipients. Titmuss refers to 'states of dependency' which are recognized as collective responsibilities (Titmuss 1955a: 42–3). These include injury, disease, disability, old age, childhood, maternity, and unemployment. Medical care is a social service because it deals with sickness; education, with children; social security, with poverty, unemployment, and old age. The difference between housing and libraries is that we classify public tenants as 'dependent' without applying the term to library users.

In many ways, this distinction is an irrational one. The prevention of disease is 'environmental health' if it involves the control of hygiene in restaurants and 'medical care' if people receive inoculations against infection. On the face of it, people are dependent if they receive important goods or services which they need and which are largely paid for by others. But refuse collection, sewers, street lighting, and roads are all fairly essential, benefit individuals, and are paid for by taxpayers or ratepayers, not necessarily the people who use them. The recipients of public services may well have made a contribution through their own rates and taxes; but so have unemployed people paid contributions for Unemployment Benefit. The difference seems to be that public services are seen as collective resources, which members of the public share. Social services are seen, rightly or wrongly, as a means of transferring resources to people who are dependent. And this implies that recipients are liable to be seen as objects of relief rather than equal participants in society.

THE WELFARE STATE

The 'welfare state' is a state which benefits its citizens in accordance with a certain set of principles, 'from cradle to grave'. Hall writes:

The distinguishing characteristic of the Welfare State is the assumption by the community, acting through the State, of the responsibility for providing the means whereby all its members can reach minimum standards of health, economic security and

civilised living, and can share according to their capacity in its social
and cultural heritage.

(Hall, quoted in Forder 1974: 2)

But the establishment of minimum standards is not enough. The
existence of a minimum only suggests that a safety net exists for
anyone who falls below a certain level – a residual concept of welfare
– and the promise of a 'welfare state' entails more than this. Briggs
outlines three ways in which the welfare state affects social relationships:

First by guaranteeing individuals and families a minimum income
irrespective of the market value of their work, or their property.
Second by narrowing the extent of insecurity by enabling individuals and families to meet certain 'social contingencies' (for
example sickness, old age and unemployment) which lead otherwise to individual or family crisis, and third, by ensuring that all
citizens without distinction of status or class are offered the best
standards available in relation to a certain agreed range of social
services.

(Briggs 1961: 228–30)

There is, in the first of these criteria, the assumption of a market
economy. The second emphasizes the idea of a social service as a
collective responsibility. Though these are necessary conditions, it is
the third criterion which actively distinguishes the 'welfare state'
from other types of welfare provision. It makes two points. One is
that the service should be at the best possible level. The other is the
principle of *universality*, that services should cover everyone. This
principle was central to the foundation of the British welfare state, as
represented in the National Health Service and the Beveridge
Report. The description of other societies as 'welfare states' – like
Sweden (Wilson 1979), or even the United States (Trattner 1974) –
depends perhaps more on quality than universality. The term has
come to apply more to social-welfare provision in practice than to the
ideals, and it is difficult to describe Britain as a 'welfare state' without
admitting others whose welfare services are equivalent or superior.

The principle of universality identifies the welfare state very much
with the idea of public services, rather than the traditional social
services. This is what distinguished the welfare state from the Poor

Law before it. Prior to 1948, services had been primarily residual – a safety net for the minority unable to cope in a competitive society. After 1948, services became *institutional*. The model of institutional welfare is based on the view that most people are likely to have a need for welfare services at some time in their lives, and that it is a social responsibility to provide for the contingencies. Dependency becomes an accepted part of social life.

Although residual and institutional models are often represented as diametrical opposites, their effective functions are basically very similar. Residual welfare is associated with activities which cure or protect the individual; but so is institutional welfare. Either model could be said to be altruistic or humanitarian; either may be seen as having a handmaiden function. Residual welfare is perhaps more associated with ideas of social control, institutional welfare with the developmental aims of welfare; but there are residual measures which have developmental functions, like Educational Maintenance Allowances to help children in poor families stay on at school, and institutional measures which have aspects of social control, like schooling. There is no necessary difference in the approach taken by the different models. They are not distinguished by their methods or their functions but by their intentions towards the people they serve. The 'welfare state' may be enlightened by a moral commitment to help all its citizens, but this is a very vague basis on which to form policies or decide about services in practice.

WELFARE STATES

Thoenes defines the welfare state as a form of society 'characterised by a system of democratic government-sponsored welfare placed on a new footing and offering a guarantee of collective social care to its citizens, concurrently with the maintenance of a capitalist system of production' (Thoenes 1966: 125). Like Thoenes, Marshall also represents the 'welfare state' as part of a complex society, allied to a capitalist market economy and a democratic political structure (Marshall 1981). Countries which fall into this category include the United Kingdom, the United States, Australia, New Zealand, and most countries in Northern and Western Europe. Countries which do not resemble it include the Soviet Union and the Eastern bloc, because they are not democratic or capitalist.

Marshall's description of 'democratic-welfare-capitalism' is based on an *ideal type* of society. An ideal type is a model, to which reality may or may not conform. This type of explanation is useful because it points up certain essential features, but it can also be misleading in certain respects. For one thing, it includes criteria which are debatable; is there any intrinsic reason why the welfare state should be capitalist? For another, the model as I have presented it fails to point to other types of comparison. It excludes, for the purposes of the argument, several important defining characteristics of the welfare state, including universality, collectivism, or an emphasis on positive freedom. These omissions do not invalidate Marshall's ideas, but the effect of the exclusion is to point to different types of comparisons from others which might have been made. The United States may resemble welfare states in some respects, but it is questionable whether its inclusion is any more valid or appropriate than the inclusion of the Soviet Union would be. A different ideal model, concentrating on collectivism, state intervention, and universality, might show the welfare state in a very different light, placing the United Kingdom in a category with the Eastern bloc. Both models would highlight certain aspects of the welfare state; both are true to some degree; but equally, both of them give only a part of the total picture.

In philosophy, the description of objects by considering their 'essential' features has largely been abandoned in favour of a different type of argument: Wittgenstein's idea of *family resemblance*. If a name applies to something, it is not because it can be compared to a model, but because it resembles other things which form some kind of group. A 'family' is a cluster of interrelated conditions. The difference between these two methods is subtle but important. If A, B, and C can all be compared to an ideal type D, they would be held to be 'essentially' the same. But the respects in which they resemble D might be different; the fact that A, B, and C are like D does not mean that A is like B or C. And the problem with an idealized model is that it can be constructed so as to include features of A, B, and C even though they have little relationship to each other when they are compared directly. Members of a 'family' might also not have much directly in common – there are 'distant relatives', members on the edge of different clusters – but they are identified as members by the actual similarities and relationships between them. The use of words to describe objects depends on the way reality is seen and the interpretation put on a variety of relationships.

A reference to a 'family' of welfare states helps, I think, to get around some of the problems. Membership of the 'family' depends not so much on three or four defining characteristics as on patterns of resemblance based on, first, expressed principles and their practical implementation and, second, the historical identification with the family. Jones offers, with apologies for oversimplification, a few 'pen-portraits' of states with different approaches to 'welfare capitalism' (Fig. 6.1). I am not sure, on this basis, exactly which countries should be included as welfare states; the family probably includes the United Kingdom and Sweden, and possibly excludes the United States, but to say even this much really requires rather more information about the systems of welfare in the different countries. This shows both the advantages and disadvantages of an approach based on 'family resemblance'; it might be less effective at crystallizing issues into convenient explanations, but it is also more accurate.

Conceptions of the welfare state are strongly rooted in history, and are linked in particular with the development of the welfare state in the United Kingdom. When Thoenes refers to welfare 'placed on a new footing', he recalls the conscious foundation of the UK welfare state in 1948. There is a danger of confusing the ideals with the reality. Robson takes issue with Thoenes's description of the welfare state as a form of 'society': 'A welfare state and a welfare society are by no means synonymous. Indeed, some of our most serious difficulties are due to the fact that we are trying to be a welfare state without being a welfare society' (Robson 1976: 11). The point is emphasized by the problems highlighted in Chapter 3. Titmuss, whose arguments can be seen as a case for a 'welfare society', objected to the idea of the 'welfare state' altogether (Titmuss 1968: Ch. 11). He disliked the complacency the term inspired – the belief it solved all problems – and the petty nationalism which it seemed to encourage, by focusing attention on welfare in one country rather than internationally. But, in addition, he felt that the idea tended to ignore the basic idea of costs. If the welfare of some people increased, the

Figure 6.1 Patterns of welfare capitalism

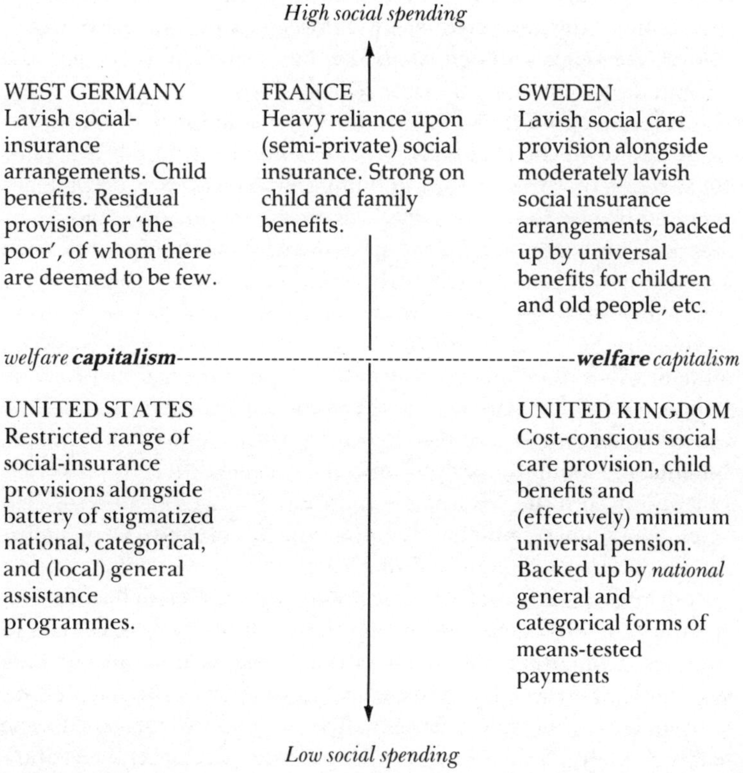

High social spending

WEST GERMANY
Lavish social-
insurance
arrangements. Child
benefits. Residual
provision for 'the
poor', of whom there
are deemed to be few.

FRANCE
Heavy reliance upon
(semi-private) social
insurance. Strong on
child and family
benefits.

SWEDEN
Lavish social care
provision alongside
moderately lavish
social insurance
arrangements, backed
up by universal
benefits for children
and old people, etc.

welfare **capitalism**--**welfare** *capitalism*

UNITED STATES
Restricted range of
social-insurance
provisions alongside
battery of stigmatized
national, categorical,
and (local) general
assistance
programmes.

UNITED KINGDOM
Cost-conscious social
care provision, child
benefits and
(effectively) minimum
universal pension.
Backed up by *national*
general and
categorical forms of
means-tested
payments

Low social spending

Source: Jones 1985: 82.

welfare of others would probably be reduced. The welfare state does not benefit 'everyone', if we mean by that 'each individual'. It benefits everyone in so far as they are members of a society, but individually, or as the members of certain groups, their interests may suffer.

THE STATE AND WELFARE

The 'state', Benn and Peters note, is commonly written of as if it really existed (Benn and Peters 1959: 252–3). But the state has no substance of its own; it cannot think, or act. It is a name attached to a group of activities, undertaken by people in a variety of settings, which we interpret as a unified structure. Raphael describes the state as an association, distinguished from others by several characteristics (Raphael 1976, Ch. 2). It has universal jurisdiction between territorial boundaries; it is omnicompetent. It is also represented as a body with supreme authority. Berki defines the state as 'an institutional structure whose primary and distinctive function is the maintenance of authority in a given territorial unit' (Berki 1979: 1). 'Authority' is not the same thing as 'coercive power'. Authority implies legitimacy; it means not just that the state does control us, but that it has a moral basis for doing so. This is a particularly important issue for welfare. If we want to justify the provision of welfare services by the state of a normative basis, it is necessary to find a normative reason why we should accept its legitimacy in this area, showing not just that welfare is morally justifiable, but that provision of welfare by the state is. The problem of legitimacy has usually been framed by political philosophers as a question of *obligation* – 'why should I obey the state?' The question, 'why should the state benefit me?' is another idea of the same coin. Both are asking about the nature and purpose of the state in relation to the individual and society.

A traditional approach to the question of legitimacy is the idea of the *social contract*, a formal agreement made by people who come together from a 'state of nature' to form a society, in order to achieve certain ends desired by all of them. The individual makes a contract with other people to become a part of society. The society contracts with a government, which is set up in order to rule it; government rests, therefore, in the consent of the people it governs. Finally, a contract is made between each new individual and a state – that is, society and government – to become a citizen. This is not intended as an historical description of how states are formed; the approach is extremely artificial. Society, not isolation, is the natural condition of mankind, government develops with society, and hardly anybody has a choice not to be governed. The point of the idea of a 'social contract' is not to examine the way things are, as Rousseau made clear (Rousseau 1762) but to provide a basis for what is legitimate, and in the past the idea has been enormously important as a challenge to the legitimacy of governments formed without popular consent. The importance of this view is that the actions of government have to be seen as a way to achieve social ends. The state is simply a mechanism through which things can be done. The provision of welfare, by this account, is not just a legitimate function of government; it is part of the basic reason why government should exist at all.

It is perhaps more convincing to argue that the state has gained legitimacy historically. Burke, in common with the contract theorists, believed that government is 'a contrivance of human wisdom to provide for human wants' (Burke 1790: 71), but saw the process as the outcome of progressive historical development. The state gains authority, Nozick argues, because a particular agency exercising force in society gains precedence over others (Nozick 1974). This 'Dominant Protection Agency' evolves into the state because of the advantages it offers people; these advantages make it acceptable, and it becomes possible to gain authority on the basis that its use of power is accepted. This process is directly equivalent to the 'prescription' of moral norms. The same argument can, of course, be extended to cover welfare provision, which has developed over time and become largely accepted in the process.

If the state did not exist, it would be necessary to invent it. Brennan and Friedman point out, I think rightly, that 'any purely ethical theory of distribution must ultimately be lodged in a theory of the institutions through which the distributional ethics are to be realised' (Brennan and Friedman 1981: 41). The provision of welfare is arguably a way of pursuing a concept of the 'common good'. But if there is a common good, there needs to be some way of trying to bring it about. Olson argues, from an economic perspective, that any rational individual, pursuing self-interested motives, has no incentive to contribute to the common good beyond a certain point (Olson 1971, Ch. 1). This is the problem of the 'free rider'. If individuals each have a choice about whether or not to pay for a social service, the rational decision of each may be to let others do so. Once this has started to happen, the cost to those who are paying will go up; provision is likely to become more and more burdensome as fewer and fewer people contribute, to the point where it will not be paid for at all. This implies either that incentives have to be created for individuals to contribute, or that some compulsion will be needed; and the use of compulsion calls for intervention by a properly constituted legitimate authority.

A number of critics argue that the authority of the state has to be limited. In the first place, even if welfare is necessary, the expansion of the state to provide it is potentially dangerous. Hayek accepts the need for some welfare provision, but sees the growth of the state as leading inexorably towards totalitarianism (Hayek 1944). Second, the provision of welfare may conflict with other principles. If a strongly individual model of freedom and property is adopted, then intervention by the state to redistribute resources may be seen as an infringement of personal liberty. Nozick argues that only the maintenance of order and arbitration of disputes can be seen as proper functions of the state: 'the minimal state is the most extensive state that can be justified' (Nozick 1974: 149). This accepts that the state does have some authority; without it, not even these minimal functions would be legitimate. But overall, Nozick's position is tenable only if individual freedom is given such a value that it overrides all the other principles which lead to welfare provision.

The third main objection to state intervention is that the case for state provision attempts to justify the means by reference to the ends. The people who criticize state activity in the field of social welfare, like Seldon (1977) and Friedman (1962), do so not necessarily because they disagree with the idea of welfare but because they think the aims can be achieved better in other ways. The argument for state provision rests as much on empirical questions as on issues of principle.

THE SOCIAL DIVISION OF WELFARE

Both the concept of the welfare state and the idea of the state as a body with universal authority within a country, conjure a picture of the state as an all-embracing, unfettered set of institutions. In reality the situation is rather more complicated than this. It is untrue, in virtually all industrialized societies, that the state has a monopoly of provision – even where there has been an attempt to impose such a monopoly (see Rein and van Gunsteren 1984). The state works within the context of diverse systems of welfare provision.

Titmuss described three main forms of welfare service: social, fiscal, and occupational (Titmuss 1955a). The first two are provided by the state; the third is private. 'Social' welfare covers the area

Table 6.1 *The mixed economy of welfare*

| Finance | Production | | | |
	Public	Private	Voluntary organizations	Informal
Public	NHS State education	Private homes for the elderly	Delegated agency services	Foster care
Private corporate	Sponsored university research	Occupational welfare	Philanthropic foundations	
Private co-operative		Personal pensions	Friendly societies	Self-help groups
Charges to consumers	Residential care for the elderly	Private health care	Housing Association rents	Childminding
Voluntary	Hospital friends	Purchase of services by voluntary organiz- ations	Shelter Mind	Family care

ordinarily considered to be within the scope of 'social services' –
mainly the direct provision of services by the state. 'Fiscal' welfare is
the process through which people benefit from tax reliefs, by not
being taxed when others are. And 'occupational' welfare concerns
benefits given by reason of a person's occupation or employment.
Titmuss presents this classification as if it were a complete description of welfare services: 'all collective interventions to meet certain
needs of the individual and/or to serve the wider interests of society
may now be broadly grouped into three major categories of welfare'
(Titmuss 1955a: 42). As a description of the organization of welfare,
however, his model has important deficiencies. He excludes the
voluntary sector, and the 'informal' sector – redistribution which
occurs through personal gifts and actions. The idea of 'occupational'
welfare seems to include benefits to employees provided as a

'handmaiden', 'perks' which are a substitute for wages, duties imposed on employers by the state (like safety checks or Statutory Sick Pay), and private insurance (like BUPA health insurance or private pensions) which may be taken up by individuals as well as by firms. In describing the role of the state, Titmuss passes over other issues. The state acts to redistribute resources in a number of ways. It provides direct social services, but it also offers indirect services – like employment exchanges, advice centres and health education – which assist individuals to manage their affairs without necessarily giving material help. It redistributes resources through the legal process – through compensation for injury, by creating and enforcing individual rights, and by creating a framework for the organization of welfare. Through its influence in economic affairs, it can increase the welfare of individuals and groups.

An alternative model of the forms of welfare provision is offered by the *mixed economy of welfare* proposed by Ken Judge, otherwise known as 'welfare pluralism'. Judge looks at different ways in which the finance and production of welfare services may be provided by different organizations (Judge and Knapp 1985). Table 6.1 is a development of his initial ideas. This approach helps to emphasize the diversity in practice of the sources and channels of welfare in society. This clearly has major implications for the role of the state. The state does not operate in isolation; rather, it acts in conjunction with a number of non-statutory organizations. Cawson outlines three ideal models of state activity (Cawson 1982, Ch. 7). In the first, the state facilitates private provision, through the creation of a legal framework which regulates activity in the market. The second model is bureaucratic: the state directs activity and provides services itself in a detailed form. Third, the state may bargain and negotiate with various organizations in order to bring about changes. The role of the state in respect of welfare in this model is to encourage and enable developments to take place in the provision of services. The commitment of the state to the provision of welfare in practice contains elements of all three roles. In the United Kingdom the state regulates the private market in areas like private rented housing or childminding. It acts to provide services directly in health care and education. It also, in practice, enters into negotiation and bargaining with interest groups in areas like occupational pensions, wage-bargaining in the public sector or inner-city 'partnership' schemes.

The term 'state intervention' implies that the state somehow comes from outside society, whereas in fact the two are inseparable. Rein points out that the state can *regulate* the private sector – that is, create rules which the private sector must follow, as it does, for example, in the licensing of nursing homes (Rein 1983). It may *mandate* the private sector, instructing it to perform certain functions. An example of this is 'Pay as You Earn', the adminis-tration of taxation and national insurance contributions by employers. The state *stimulates* certain types of provision for example by offering certain tax reliefs and incentives. Charities usually enjoy major tax concessions. And it may *support* the private sector, by undertaking to rescue it financially in the event of difficulties: a guarantee of this kind has been given to occupational pensions in the United Kingdom. Support, in practice, goes far beyond this; as the table of the 'mixed economy of welfare' suggests, the provision of finance by the state is used to such an extent that it becomes difficult to separate state and private-sector activity in any meaningful sense.

This clearly reflects on the idea of the 'welfare state' in practice. The ideas of the 'welfare state' and 'welfare society' tend to give the impression of a cosy, all-embracing network of provision. The principle of the welfare state is important because it prompts attempts to ensure that services do meet the needs of everyone. But the reality is more a hodge-podge of different organizations concerned with the provision of welfare, in which the institutions of the state play a major part. This, in turn, reflects on the values that are associated with the welfare state. Rein argues not only that values and principles affect the provision of services, but that the converse is true – the structure of services changes principles by affecting the context in which values are formed and the ways in which problems are interpreted. There is a strong case to be made out for this position. The curious limitations put on the idea of 'social welfare', the identification of the 'welfare state' with the sort of services which developed in the United Kingdom and elsewhere, the relationship of the state to society, are all conditioned by historical experience; and an understanding of their application relies at least as much on descriptions of what actually happens as it does on the analysis of principles and theories of social welfare.

VII

Democracy

Summary: *Democracy is government by the people governed, or at least by a majority. The majority represents either a consensus view, or coalitions of interests, but the interests of minorities are protected through liberal rights. Conventionally, democracy means representative government, but the main justification for democracy is self-determination, and this has led in social policy to an emphasis on participation.*

Democracy is government 'of the people, for the people, and by the people'. Government, or rule, is the act of making decisions through the institutions of the state which affect oneself or others. All government, of course, is government *of* people. The view that government is *for* people – or in their interests – is closely linked with the idea of the welfare state, which helps to explain why the welfare state is thought of as being 'democratic'. But government 'for the people' is not a distinctive characteristic of democracy. Thomas Hobbes stated, in the seventeenth century, that the central principle of all government was '*salus populi suprema est lex*' – 'the welfare of the people is the highest law' – but argued nevertheless that this could best be achieved through a benevolent despotism (Hobbes 1651). The feature that sets democracy apart from other forms of government is that it is done *by* the people. And government 'by the people' is not necessarily a guarantee of their welfare. There is a presumption that people are likely to want what is good for them, but as the argument in Chapter 1 suggests, the satisfaction of wants is only a part of welfare. Much of the case for democracy is a case for self-determination and depends on the view that people are themselves the best judges of their own interests.

Government 'by the people' is an ideal, but it is an ideal which is interpreted in several different ways; scarcely a country in the world does not lay claim to be 'democratic'. Lively gives a number of definitions of 'rule by the people' (Lively 1975). It may imply that everyone actually governs, or is involved in governing. It may mean that the rulers are accountable to the people – that decisions can be corrected, altered or at least effectively objected to by people who have some sanction - or accountable to the people's representatives. In some democracies, rulers are chosen by the people or their representatives. (Governors may be chosen without being account- able subsequently: Lively argues that this is insufficient for democ- racy.) Lastly, rule may be in the interests of the people – that is, 'for' them. This does not clearly distinguish a democracy from any other form of government and is again inadequate.

If 'the people' is seen as a group of individuals, each with his or her own desires or beliefs, then government 'by the people' is a means for them to put their different views and to satisfy their wants. If 'the people' is a collective entity – like 'society' – government by the people implies that people should act with a common purpose. Rousseau writes of a *general will*, directed towards achieving a common good (Rousseau 1762). The idea of a general will is an artificial one, even if we do tend at times to say that 'society' or 'the people' approve certain policies: there is no collective mind. But even though there may be conflicts of interest between members of society, it may be possible to talk of a 'common good': it can be identified with the later concepts of social welfare discussed in Chapter 1, and it is subject to the same reservations. The main objection to Rousseau's argument, though, is that it assumes people really 'want' what is good for them rather than what they might say they want. It boils down to rule in the interests of the people – a position which is questionably democratic.

The idea of the people as 'sovereign' is collective in form; it means that all authority is derived from them, usually by means of the popular vote. Referenda – votes by the public on specific issues – are not in general use. However, in Britain the idea of the election 'mandate' has become important. A party which seeks election puts forward a manifesto of its policies. It receives the votes of a majority – or, more precisely, gains a majority of seats, which, in the United Kingdom at least, is not at all the same thing – and then claims a mandate from the electorate for those activities it has said it will undertake. This claim is questionable even for those policies which have been major issues in election campaigns. A vote for a party may relate to its general approach, its image, the individuals who form part of it, or other policies in the package the party has offered. It certainly cannot be taken as approval of all the policies the party pursues. For issues which tend to be relatively minor in electoral terms – like questions concerning the reform of social-security benefits or value for money in health services – the claim is altogether untenable. A government which is elected through a process accepted as democratic can claim some legitimacy on that ground, but this is not the same as saying it is doing what people want.

Elections in general depend on a principle of majority rule. There are a number of justifications for the tradition. One argument is that the view of the majority is the best available representation of a consensus – that is, of shared opinions and wants. And even if some people disagree, counting heads, as Fitzjames Stephen once commented, is better than breaking them. But this is a dangerous principle, because it could subject the minority to the tyranny of the majority. The isolation of mentally ill people from the community, or the former segregation of racial minorities in schools in the United States, could be justified in terms of a majority view, despite the effect they have had on individuals.

A more subtle view, and one which I think better represents attitudes to democracy in Britain and the United States, is that the majority vote represents successful coalitions of interests. Madison, one of the founders of the American Union, argued that as long as there were no permanent factions to give one group consistent rule over others, majority voting would effectively take into account all citizens' views. 'It is of great importance in a republic', he wrote,

> not only to guard the society against the oppression of its rulers, but to guard one part of the society against the injustice of the other part. Different interests necessarily exist in different classes of citizens. If a majority be united by a common interest, the rights of the minority will be insecure. There are but two methods of providing against this evil: the one by creating a will in the community independent of the majority – that is, of the society itself; the other, by comprehending in the society so many separate

descriptions of citizens as will render an unjust combination of a
majority on the whole very improbable, if not impracticable.

(*Federalist Papers* 51 [1788]: 311)

Benn and Peters suggest that an essential element of democracy is
that 'every claim should be given a hearing' (Benn and Peters 1959:
354). This is necessary to ensure both groups are able to form
coalitions. It emphasizes the link between the concept of democracy
and rights; the common understanding of 'democracy' in the West is
a liberal democracy in which rights are safeguarded. The extension
of these rights to include welfare is not inherent in the concept of
democracy, but Marshall's idea of 'citizenship' closely identifies
democracy with rights and the 'welfare state'; the provision of
welfare is in the citizen's interests and necessary for participation in
society.

This is an idealistic position. Alternative theories of democracy
have tried to reflect, more accurately, what actually happens. The
case for majority rule is that it provides a convenient convention, to
create an accountable form of government that will respect people's
rights and protect their interests. The function of a democracy, by
this argument, is to elect representatives who decide, not according
to the will of the electors but according to their interests, and who are
accountable for their actions at elections. Schumpeter describes this
as a competition between élite groups who wish to form a government. 'The democratic method', he writes, 'is that institutional
arrangement for arriving at political decisions in which individuals
acquire the power to decide by means of a competitive struggle for
the people's vote' (Schumpeter 1967: 173). The competing factions
accept the legitimacy of the election as a mechanism to determine
who should be in power, and order their affairs so as to capture a
majority of votes. This means that they attempt both to distinguish
their policies from the other group while at the same time trying to
hold the middle ground.

This is an attractive theory, because it seems to explain the way
representative government works in terms which can easily be
applied to the United Kingdom and the United States. Its main
weaknesses lie in its very simplicity. It does not clearly explain, for
example, the workings of multi-party democracies, ideas like the

'mandate', parliamentary traditions, or the role of individual politicians as constituency representatives. But it does offer certain
predictions about the way in which parties are likely to behave. They
will produce packages of policies, not so much to promise specific
improvements a to show they offer a credible alternative in government. They are, then, as likely to emphasize approach, image, and
past successes – seeking to distinguish themselves from their
opponents – as ways of attracting votes. Welfare issues are likely to be
included in the package, but they are not necessarily central to the
party's platform. Social welfare is liable to be, as a result, peripheral
to the electoral process.

The decisions made in the area of social policy reflect less, then, the
wishes of the people than the priorities of politicians, subject to
pressure from organized lobbies, the influence of the media, the
legal system, the administration, and the arguments of 'experts' in
the field. Banting gives illustrations of these influences in case studies
of housing, social security, and education policy in the 1960s
(Banting 1979). He traces out five stages in the process of policy-
making: the awareness of the problem, its salience (or prominence);
its definition; specification of alternatives; and the choice between
alternatives. This is a useful model because it draws attention at each
stage to various influences on policy and issues of interpretation.

An example might be the revision of practice in child-abuse cases
which followed the inquiry into the death of Maria Colwell (DHSS
1974). She was a child who was returned to her 'natural' family – her
mother and stepfather – from foster care, and subsequently died
after months of neglect. Many agencies had known something about
her condition, but they had not put together the information that
could have led to action to save her. Public and political awareness of
the problem was created through her death; its salience was
determined by a committee of inquiry and, more important, the
attention of the press. The problem was defined in the press not as an
issue of abuse by the responsible adults but of negligence by social
workers. The alternatives specified, as a result, mainly concerned the
practice of agencies. Measures which were not really considered were
a massive injection of central funds into child care, greater deterrent
penalties for carers, abolition of corporal punishment in the home or
the extension of children's rights against carers; these were not ways

in which the problem was interpreted. The choices made at the local level included tightening up of supervision of families, increased supervision of social workers at work, a greater priority given to child abuse relative to other responsibilities, and new arrangements for service co-ordination; at the national level there was a Children Act which introduced new forms of guardianship. However reasonable in themselves, these measures later proved manifestly inadequate to stem the tide of abuse.

Banting's model is descriptive rather than analytical. It helps to tease out the stages of the process, but it does not explain why certain measures achieve prominence when others do not. It is not enough for a 'need' to be recognized for some response to be made. There is, for example, a clear 'need' at present in the United Kingdom for services for single homeless people, but these services are not generally provided by the state (the government is currently seeking to withdraw even from the little commitment it has), and their housing is left to voluntary work and administrative discretion. Before anything is done, a 'need' has to be translated into an issue. Hall *et al.* attribute the prominence of issues to three factors; legitimacy, support and feasibility (Hall *et al.* 1975). 'Legitimacy' means that a measure is accepted in principle, at least by those responsible for decisions. 'Support' means that the measure is promoted by people who are in a position to exercise pressure in its behalf. (It does not necessarily mean 'electoral' support.) 'Feasibility' means that a policy must be practicable. It is arguable whether prominence does depend on practicality; some measures passed in social policy could be described as wholly unrealistic. In the United States, for example, old people have a number of rights in law, including a right to respect, which are quite unenforceable (Bergman, in ICSW 1969: 430). And in the United Kingdom, the Chronically Sick and Disabled Persons Act 1970 was passed even though there were no resources made available to fulfil the obligations it created. The argument made by its supporters was that resources could be made available in time; the important thing was to accept the principle (Gould and Topliss 1981). But the question of priority has become of much greater importance in a time of economic stringency. It is not enough for a problem to be known, recognized, accepted as a legitimate ground for action; it must also be more salient, more legitimate, more effectively supported than other issues with which it is competing for attention. This depends crucially on the relative degree of support in comparison to other aims. Because economic issues tend to have a pre-eminent position over social issues, social policy is usually conditional on resources.

The political process this describes is familiar and widely accepted as a legitimate form of government; it seems, for the most part, to work. But it is debatable whether it has much to do with 'democracy' at all. Perhaps the demands of legitimacy and support indicate that the process does protect people's interests. But even if it does protect people's interests – and not everyone believes that it does – rule in people's interests is not the same as rule by them.

DEMOCRACY AND SELF-DETERMINATION

Benjamin Constant, a French liberal philosopher, argued that there was a part of each individual which was his or her concern, and no-one else's. Equally, there was a part of every relationship which was private to the people concerned. This principle extended to small groups, large groups, communities, and regions (Constant 1815). This argument links self-determination with local autonomy and national independence.

Social services are often administered at the local level. In Britain, schools, housing, and personal social services are the preserve of local government. Local government used also to be responsible for health and social security, but it lost them after the Second World War to central government. (It has also lost its responsibilities for gas, water, electricity, much of its control over police and fire services, and its ability to control its own finances has been substantially restricted. It seems fair to say that local government in Britain is in decline.)

In theory, local government has four great advantages over central government. First, it gives people in a local community a greater degree of collective autonomy than central control does. Second, because each person has a larger say in local government than in national government, it is more accountable. Third, it is less remote from the people who are being governed, and so more responsive. Fourth, it is more democratic, because it creates a forum in which certain activities which are overshadowed on the national stage can become a part of political debate. However, local government in Britain falls some way short of this ideal. Local government elections do not attract a great deal of interest, and voting patterns tend to have more to do with national party politics than with local issues. This reduces the immediate accountability of local representatives for their actions. Flexibility and autonomy are limited. There is a wide range of central government controls which limit its discretion – largely, but not solely, through financial mechanisms and the statutory definition of the powers of the local authority. Central government can prevent local government from pursuing certain activities. Local government has enough autonomy to hold back the pace of central government by dragging its feet for a while, but open defiance is unusual. As for responsiveness, local government areas are probably too large for them to be genuinely sensitive to the needs of small communities within their boundaries, and although it is possible at least to provide services in a small neighbourhood, the controlling body can be as remote from these communities in practice as central government is from its local offices.

The inadequacy of existing structures has been at the root of much of the trend to 'participation' in the social services. Participation returns to a view of democracy as involving people – clients, consumers, workers, and 'communities' – directly in the decision-making process. The movement stems from three main sources: the ancient ideal of democracy, taken up in the early part of this century by 'syndicalists', who believed in workers' control; the fear of bureaucracy identified by Hayek (1944); and the breakdown of deference towards the 'experts' who ran services like housing, planning, and transport. It was in the area of planning that participation developed most strongly in Britain. Damer and Hague give several reasons for this trend (Damer and Hague 1971). In part the policy developed through an imitation of trends in the United States. There was an increased public interest in conservation. Delays in the previous system were caused by active and litigious protesters, who had caused developments to grind to a halt. Planning had become recognized as a political activity. It was the forum for groups of articulate, well-resourced, and politically adept middle-class communities to make their case – the delay of construction of a third

London airport for over twenty years is a splendid illustration – and the principle of 'examination in public' (DoE 1969) became institutionalized in recognition of the fact that policies had become unworkable without it.

The case for participation, Richardson argues, is both that it enhances the personal abilities of the participants and that it is instrumental to decision-making (Richardson 1983, Ch. 4). It is developmental because it gives people a sense of control over their lives; it educates them about politics and policies; it gives opportunities for self-expression; it makes it possible to identify and act in the participants' interests, or at least according to their expressed wants. Participation facilitates decision-making by aiding mutual understanding between parties; it makes for efficiency by helping to match policies to goals, and by producing consent at the initial stages; it diffuses the distribution of power, of which more shortly; and it protects the people who are affected by the decisions. Against this, it can be argued that participation may be unrepresentative, favouring activists rather than everyone who has an interest. It is very time-consuming. (Some tenants' co-operatives make a large feature of attendance at meetings – in fact, people may not be allocated houses if they don't go. This seems to me an intolerable burden to place on people who don't otherwise have a sufficient choice as to their accommodation; there are far more important things to do with an evening.)

Perhaps most important, the emphasis on participation fails to recognize that there may be a conflict of interest, where one party must lose. It has become fashionable, in the provision of council housing, to favour greater participation by tenants. Colin Ward, for example, has argued for the power of tenants to run their own estates; he cites the example of Oslo, where he argues that many of the problems associated with council housing in the United Kingdom do not arise because tenants have the power to affect their environment (Ward 1974). Ann Power, drawing from experience in Holloway Tenants Co-op and Tulse Hill, claims that the success of many special management projects depends on the extent to which tenants are able to affect their own environments (Power 1981). This is an understandable reaction to the bureaucratic and paternalistic approach of many local authority housing departments, and the emphasis on participation is based on a laudable attempt to overcome some of these disadvantages through collective action. However, as Craddock points out, the effects of participative schemes may be actually to reduce the power of minority opinions within the tenant group, and participation may give tenants power at the expense of others (Craddock 1975: 23). The effect may be to set some disadvantaged poor people, the tenants, against others who are less well organized. Council tenants are not the only group whose interests need to be protected. They are major protagonists in a competition for scarce resources; their interests are clearly and strongly opposed to many of the people who want to move into council housing. Many tenants hope, quite reasonably, to improve their housing status by transferring to a better area. Many applicants for rehousing are the sons and daughters of council tenants, living with them while waiting for accommodation, and tenants are more likely to favour their claims over others who want council housing. This means that people outside the council sector are very likely to be put at a major disadvantage in the competition for resources. This includes people in private tenancies, owner-occupiers of unsatisfactory housing, and people from outside the area; the groups who will be excluded are likely to include, amongst others, racial minorities, victims of domestic violence in private accommodation, and people discharged from mental institutions.

Arnstein describes a 'ladder of citizen participation', ranging from manipulation and 'therapy' to informing, consulting, placating, partnership, delegated power, and ultimately, citizen control (Arnstein 1971). This sees participation very much in terms of a conflict between 'us' (the community) and 'them' (those in charge). But many decisions are based on other types of conflict. The decision is retained by politicians and adminstrators in order to protect one group against another. In practice, the role of 'them' may be to arbitrate where there is a clash of interests and participatory democracy is unable to provide a satisfactory answer.

DEMOCRACY AND WELFARE

It is possible to identify a number of elements in democratic theory which are linked with a commitment to welfare. The idea that government should be in the interests of the people governed is fundamental to both. The view that people are the best judges of their own interests (a view which not everybody shares) implies that some mechanism is needed which allows them to decide – though there is a significant difference between saying that people are individually the best judges of their own interests and that they are collectively the best judges. The emphasis on personal development, self-determination, and education for responsibility and independence are aims which welfare services may share. But none of these really accounts for the strength of the links between the ideas, and the close identification of democracy with 'welfare' and 'the welfare state' seems tenuous. More important, I think, is the historical association of concepts of democracy with rights, citizenship, and accountability. Without these principles, democracy would be worthless. The things that matter about a democracy have little to do with the traditional ideal.

A number of problems stem from the emphasis on the ideal. There may be more stress on the form – the authority of someone who is 'democratically elected', the expression of views as representing 'the community' or 'the majority' – than on the substance, whether rights are being respected and whose interests a measure is in. Policies may be more concerned with 'democracy' than rights to welfare – the election of parent governors to schools, or the creation of Tenants Consultative Committees, are no guarantee that the people affected will have any redress. And concentration on models of democracy may lead to a distortion of perception as to how decisions are actually made. Some critics suggest that the claim to be 'democratic' may become a means to legitimize policies in the interests of a few. This position is considered further in the next chapter.

VIII

Power

Summary: *Elitist models suggest that power is concentrated in relatively few hands, and welfare is used partly to control recipients. Marxist analyses, which are more complex, argue that hegemony is exercised by a dominant class, with the result that society is organized in the interests of that class. Neo-marxists have argued that welfare provision is necessary for the system of economic production, but there is a tension between the two, leading to crisis. However, Marxism has a limited explanatory potential in this context. Explanations in terms of 'power' are unnecessary; inequalities in welfare provision arise simply from the failure of policies to address existing inequalities in society.*

The institutions of the state are defined by their power and authority, and it is a primary function of the state to exercise power over other organizations, as well as over individual citizens. The use of some degree of power is virtually implicit in the process of redistribution. If one person is to benefit at the expense of another, and this is not done voluntarily by charity, then some mechanism must exist through which redistribution can be effected. However, such 'mechanisms' are not necessarily neutral between the parties; the use of power becomes problematic because it can be seen as serving the interests of some at the expense of others.

The understanding of power depends crucially, then, on its distribution in society. The distribution of power is commonly represented in one of two basic models, *élitist* and *pluralist* approaches. In élitist models, power is concentrated in the hands of a few; in pluralist models, it is diffused and held by many. The simplest model of a concentration of power uses the idea of a *ruling élite*, a fairly small cadre of people able to make all the important decisions which affect other people's lives. The argument is clearly difficult to sustain in a complex industrial society, simply because of the number of decisions which would have to be made. This complexity has brought writers about élites to identify them in specific defined areas. Wright Mills posits three fairly distinct ruling élites: economic, political, and military (1956). Bottomore refers to bureaucratic and aristocratic élites (1966); Keller adds social and religious ones (1963); Lee identifies further élites at a local level (1963).

Corporatist views interpret the exercise of power as the domination of established corporate interests. Schmitter describes a corporatist society as one dominated by 'a limited number of singular, compulsory, non-competitive, hierarchically ordered and functionally differentiated categories' (Schmitter, quoted in Ham and Hill 1984: 37–8). The most important term here is 'hierarchical'; in a hierarchical structure, it is possible to direct things from above. This represents corporatism as a mechanism through which élite rule can be maintained. But there is also a view of corporatism which views the different corporations as élite factions in conflict. Galbraith argues that as society becomes more complex, and in particular as industrial processes become more advanced technologically, decisions must be taken by groups of people each with special areas of interest or expertise (Galbraith 1972). (This has the interesting side-effect, he suggests, that corporate interests press for public spending on high technology in order to maintain their industrial output. The main area in which the trend occurs is in military expenditure, but the same pattern arguably exists in expenditure on health services.)

As the number of factions increases, the idea comes more and more to resemble pluralist ideas. Pluralism is distinguished from élitism, not by the view that conflicts do not occur, but rather through the view that policy is made through a process of interaction between many disparate elements. Although there may be a tendency for the forms of power to be concentrated in relatively few hands – no-one believes that power is distributed equally – it tends to be diffused. This is not directly equivalent to formal democracy, because the analysis of decision-making depends on factors beyond the election of governments; power is spread across a wide range of interest groups. However, Dahl identifies pluralism closely with democracy, following Madison's view that diversity is necessary in a democracy to prevent one faction becoming dominant over others (Dahl 1956).

Individuals have little say, except as part of organized interest groups. But if society is open, politics are fluid, and many different types of groups are involved in decision-making, the effect is very close to democratic government. Although Dahl's argument is presented in an abstract and idealized form, the implication is clear that pluralism is one of the major elements that makes the United States more democratic than other countries.

The emphasis on power in studies of welfare represents a challenge to the assumption that social services are designed to increase the well-being of the people who receive them. Elite theory implies that policy is likely to be made in the interests of those in power. There are cases in which welfare services have explicit objectives which favour the preservation of the status quo, like Bismarck's introduction of social insurance in Germany. 'If you do not give the people social reform', Quintin Hogg argued in the Parliamentary debate on the Beveridge Report, 'they are going to give you social revolution' (Hansard, vol. 386, col. 1918). Another example is the introduction of council housing in 1919, which was strongly influenced by the fear of a Bolshevik revolution and interpreted in the light of a strike by munitions workers during wartime on account of housing conditions (see Orbach 1977). But open statements of this type are rare, and even in the cases where they are made, whatever the other motives associated with them, national insurance and council housing clearly offered a real benefit to the recipients. Tawney, a socialist, describes the idea that welfare services can be seen as palliatives as 'claptrap' (Tawney 1931: 120).

The idea of 'social control' is closely linked with this kind of analysis. The term is often used ambiguously, drifting from the issues of morality and deviance to the use of power by a ruling class; the connection between them is that the conformity and social stability emphasized by social norms are seen as working in the interests of the dominant class, removing any threat to their pre-eminence. Higgins outlines several different models of control (Higgins 1980). There is the maintenance of social order through norms and values, described by Janowitz, which she calls social control by 'self-determination' (Janowitz 1976). There are pressures for conformity, paternalistic policies, and 'integration' - the adjustment of the individual to the environment idealistically recommended by Boulding and Titmuss. There is 'co-optation', the defusing of protest by involving people in decision-making, which is described in Arnstein's 'ladder of participation'. And there are more extreme forms of social control: Piven and Cloward argue, for example, that

> to buttress weak market controls and ensure the availability of marginal labour, an outcast class – the dependent poor – is created by the relief system. . . . Its degradation at the hands of relief officials serves to celebrate the value of all work.
> (Piven and Cloward 1971: 165)

In other words, they believe that welfare is being deliberately used to identify people as deviant and to discourage them from dependence. The overt objectives of welfare may be humanitarian; in practice, they conceal mechanisms designed to enforce conformity and to protect the interests of employers. The system, Ginsburg argues, is 'designed to discipline claimants and to promote the values of insurance and individual and family self-help' (Ginsburg 1979: 104). There are certainly measures associated with social services which directly involve control. For example, Unemployment Benefit may be suspended for a period if a person is considered to be unemployed 'voluntarily' without 'just cause' or through 'misconduct' (a term mainly applied to people who have been sacked). However, this is a long way from saying that the welfare services are *about* control; welfare provisions may pull in contradictory directions. The issue is not that social services generally control people, but that welfare provision can be spoiled by the use of power in a way which works against the interests of the recipients.

Power is not necessarily exercised overtly, and as a result its use may be difficult to detect. Bachrach and Baratz refer to negative, 'non-decisions'. Non-decisions involve the maintenance of the status quo through 'a decision that results in the suppression or thwarting of a latent or manifest challenge to the values or interests of the decision-maker' (Bachrach and Baratz 1970: 44). This happens in several ways. There may be the use of force or intimidation to prevent a less powerful group from making a claim. Individuals may be stigmatized; the act of demanding services is seen as 'scrounging', and publicly attacked. Even where concessions seem to be made, the dominant members of society are able to maintain their position.

Concessions are subject to delay, by the construction of legal and administrative obstacles, or by prolonging discussion of proposals. Rewards are given to those who conform to the dominant norms, and those who do not conform are deprived of resources. The illustration the authors offer of this process is the treatment of blacks calling for urban renewal in the United States. Another illustration might be the treatment of social-security claimants. There is a large failure of take-up; some of it is attributable to ignorance, some to the complexity of claiming, and some to stigma. The present government argues that a reluctance to claim shows a proper sense of pride and independence, which should not be undermined. This, and the maintenance of a cumbersome administrative structure which costs claimants a great deal in time and trouble, can be seen as a form of 'non-decision-making'.

Lenin used a similar argument to emphasize the role of the state as an instrument of class oppression. Democracy, he wrote, is a sham:

> Democracy for an insignificant minority, democracy for the rich – that is the democracy of capitalist society. If we look more closely into the machinery of capitalist democracy, we see everywhere, in the "petty" – supposedly petty – details of the suffrage (residential qualification, exclusion of women, etc.), in the technique of the representative institutions, in the actual obstacles to the right of assembly (public buildings are not for "paupers"!), in the purely capitalist organisation of the daily press, etc., etc. – we see restriction after restriction upon democracy. These restrictions, exceptions, exclusions, obstacles for the poor seem slight, especially in the eyes of one who has never known want himself and has never been in close contact with the oppressed classes in their mass life . . . but in their sum total these restrictions exclude and squeeze the poor from politics, from active participation in democracy.
>
> (Lenin 1918: 80)

Lenin describes the state as 'an instrument for the exploitation of the oppressed class' (*ibid.*: 13). But it can equally be argued that the disadvantages of those who are powerless continue, not because they are deliberately maintained, but because they are not effectively addressed. They can be interpreted in structural terms – as the outcome of a social system.

MARXIST ANALYSES

In Marx's view, the 'substructure' of society is its economic foundation, which provides a basis for the political and social relationships
of the 'superstructure'. The 'ruling class' are those who own and
control the means of production. This does not mean that they 'rule'
by sitting down together to make decisions; the Marxian concept of
class unifies people according to their shared interests, and they 'rule'
in the sense that they establish the conditions in which government
operates.

The maintenance, or 'reproduction', of the social system is
determined through *hegemony*. Russell refers to power as 'the
production of intended effects' (Russell 1960: 25). But this, Lukes
argues, is not altogether adequate, because people do not have to
wait to be instructed (Lukes 1978). Hegemony is a process through
which social perceptions and values are shaped, influenced, and
ultimately determined in favour of the dominant class. Finch
describes a number of ways in which the education system 'reproduces' the social system (Finch 1984, Ch. 6). It maintains it by
educating and training the labour force. It reinforces the class
structure, by stressing the division of labour and continuity of
occupations between generations. It educates people into sexual
divisions. It socializes people into the dominant culture and the
virtues of the political order.

'The executive of the modern State', Marx wrote, 'is but a
committee for managing the common affairs of the whole bourgeoisie' (Marx 1848: 82); their interests are dominant. Miliband makes
the case that this stems from the values of those in government,
coupled with the constraints placed on government by the industrial
system (Miliband 1969). Poulantzas, by contrast, argues that the state
is not necessarily the primary source of power in society, and that it
reflects the conflict of different classes, and of factions within classes
– which means that there are likely to be inconsistencies, or
'contradictions', in the measures which the state takes:

The State organises and reproduces class hegemony by establishing a variable field of compromises between the dominant and
dominated classes; quite frequently, this will even involve the

imposition of certain short-term material sacrifices on the dominant classes. . . . It should never be forgotten that a whole series of
economic measures . . . were imposed on the State by the struggle
of the dominated classes. These struggles revolved around what
may be designated by the socially and historically determinate
notion of popular "needs": from social security to policies in
relation to unemployment and the entire field of collective
consumption. . . . But . . . all measures taken by the capitalist State,
even those imposed by the popular masses, are in the last analysis
inserted in a pro-capitalist strategy or are compatible with the
expanded reproduction of capital.

(Poulantzas 1978: 184–5)

Marxists usually see the provision of services, not as a veiled form of
repression, but as the outcome of a conflict between capital and
labour – a conflict in which neither side wholly wins or loses but in
which capital, through the process of hegemony, maintains the
upper hand.

Recent writings, attempting to modify conventional Marxist positions, have examined ways in which welfare provision helps to
maintain order. They emphasize the role of welfare in legitimizing
the existing social system, and supplement this with aspects of control
and reproduction. Ginsburg argues that welfare 'is essential in its
detailed functioning to asserting the command of capital over labour
and in its general ideological existence to securing the loyalty to the
state of the working class (Ginsburg 1979: 12). Saunders, writing
about the 'local state', refers to

Maintenance of order and social cohesion
    . . . through the support of the 'surplus population' (e.g. social
    services, and other welfare support services such as temporary
    accommodation)
    . . . through support of the agencies of legitimation (e.g. schools,
    social work, 'public participation').

(Saunders 1979: 148)

Effectively, this analysis dismisses many of the idealistic and moral
views of welfare considered up to now.

Welfare provision also serves industry through the process which
Offe calls 'commodification', helping to create conditions in which

commodities which can be traded in the economic market (Offe 1984). O'Connor writes that 'the function of the welfare system is not only to control the surplus population politically but also to expand demand and domestic markets' (O'Connor 1973: 150–1). Saunders points to

> Sustenance of private production and capital accumulation
> . . . by aiding the reorganisation and restructuring of production in space (e.g. planning and urban renewal)
> . . . through the provision of investment in "human capital" (e.g. education in general and technical college education in particular)
> . . . through 'demand orchestration' (e.g. local authority public works contracts).
>
> (Saunders 1979: 147)

and Habermas emphasizes the role of the state in creating conditions for the 'realisation' of capital, for example:

> through improvement of the material infrastructure (transportation, education, health, recreation, housing construction, etc.); . . .
> – through heightening the productivity of human labour (general system of education, vocational schools, programs for training and re-education, etc.);
> – through relieving the material costs resulting from private production (unemployment compensation, welfare, repair of ecological damage).
>
> (Habermas 1976: 35)

Commodification stresses the importance of private production, the creation of conditions for the accumulation of capital, and the imposition of constraints on the costs. Equally, though, Offe argues that welfare has certain functions which fall outside the market, requiring 'decommodification' to compensate for the problems which arise from production, to reproduce society, and to legitimize the system: 'a supportive framework of non-commodified institutions is necessary for an economic system that utilises labour power as if it were a commodity' (Offe 1984: 263). However, the attempt to maintain welfare services is beyond the financial capacity of states.

This implies a 'contradiction', or tension, between commodification and decommodification. Habermas argues that 'The government budget . . . is burdened with the public expenses of an increasingly socialised production' (Habermas 1984: 144), and Offe concludes that 'while capitalism cannot coexist *with*, neither can it exist *without*, the welfare state' (Offe 1984: 153).

But whether it is true or not that welfare has become a burden on the economy – which is debatable – it is difficult to see why, in Marxist terms, states should maintain expenditure which is not necessary to maintain the productivity of labour power. If labour is being treated as nothing but a commodity, why, for example, should any state bother to provide extensive support for people in old age, after workers have ceased to be productive? It is hardly enough to dismiss this as another aspect of 'legitimation'. There are other ways of dealing with old people, besides state pensions and medical services, which might also be 'legitimate' – like private pension arrangements, encouraging personal saving for old age, an emphasis on the duties of families to support their elders, or perhaps encouraging workers to smoke so that they drop dead at 65. Similarly, provision for mental handicap or physical disability is difficult to justify in productive terms. There comes a point at which 'legitimation', if taken far enough, cannot be regarded as merely instrumental. If legitimacy is gained through acting in people's interests, a state which devotes a high proportion of its resources to the welfare of its citizens *is* more legitimate than one which does not.

The strength of the neo-Marxist argument is that it does contribute an explanation of some functions which welfare may serve. The Marxist case is an elaborate one, though the outline given here represents only a part of a much more comprehensive set of theories of society. It offers one means of interpreting a complex situation. There are many contentious assertions in Marxism: that the development of society depends on an economic base; that social relationships are principally determined by relations between producers; that the primary relationships in society are exploitative; that those who own the means of production control them; that the economic system is fundamentally unstable; and that the system must collapse through a process of progressive immiseration leading to revolution. These arguments, however, are beyond the scope of this book. (They are examined critically in, e.g., Popper 1945, Chs. 13–17; Crosland 1956, especially Chs. 3, 8).

In the context of the analysis of welfare, Marxism has several weaknesses. First, there is a tendency to be simplistic. The Marxist view relies on a basic division between two classes and interprets evidence of the growing complexity of power structures and changes in society as basically superficial. Second, it suffers from many of the weaknesses of functionalist analysis; there is a tendency to assume that the parts are consistent with each other, and that the pieces fit. Often they do not. Third, Marxism relies on an interpretation of circumstances which may be valid in certain respects but leaves little room for other equally plausible perspectives on welfare – perspectives which describe welfare variously as humanitarian, pluralistic, or based in a developing concept of citizenship. This is a form of tunnel vision. Welfare is complex, and any adequate explanation of its functions has to be diverse. Fourth, the consistent emphasis on the negative aspects of welfare provision is not only one-sided but also, I think, morally suspect; the representation of welfare provision as 'legitimization' or 'commodification' implies that there is something reprehensible about measures which make people's lives better. Fifth, the Marxist literature, like the analytical political theory referred to in the first chapter, is often remote from reality, and it can be extremely obscure. There is a great deal of dogmatic assertion, with no consideration of other views, and the evidence used is highly selective if there is any evidence at all.

Lastly, much of what is written is only obliquely relevant to welfare problems. Issues like child abuse, mental handicap, or homelessness receive cursory attention at best. It is possible to adopt a perspective on social problems and policies from a Marxist framework, and work is beginning to appear which does so: Chris Jones, for example, in a Marxist analysis of social work, suggests that the prevention of child abuse is intended to save money by keeping children out of residential care, preventing the waste of 'human assets', and perhaps by 'reducing the problem of high-cost citizens' (Jones 1983: 13–20). But this is a long way from being a full treatment of the issue. Some welfare services simply fall outside the ambit of issues to which Marxist explanations are principally addressed.

SOCIAL CLASS AND SOCIAL WELFARE

In the context of writings about social policy, one of the main reasons for referring to 'power' is to help explain the distribution of things which lead to welfare. Some people are relatively privileged, and have a substantial command over resources; others are deprived and disadvantaged. The pattern is not by any means random.

Social relationships are structured in terms of a person's roles. A *role* describes both what a person does socially and what others expect that person to do. In many cases, a person's roles are interlinked, so that one role implies another. An occupational role, like being a doctor, implies certain other social roles. This is the basis of social *status*. Status, Marshall writes, 'covers all behaviour which society expects of a person in his capacity as occupant of the position, and also appropriate reciprocal behaviour of others towards him' (Marshall 1963: 186). But a status conveys expectations which are far beyond the immediate demands of a person's occupation. Doctors may be expected to behave with a certain amount of probity, but it would also be surprising to find them living in council housing, though this has nothing to do with the obligations of the occupation. Status implies more, then, than a set of roles; it is a structured form of social identity.

Weber writes that status is 'in the main conditioned as well as expressed through a specific style of life' (Weber 1967: 31–2). A person's life-style is a function not only of expectations but of economic power, or *class*. Classes are 'groups of people, who, from the standpoint of specific interests, have the same economic position' (*ibid.*). If welfare is seen in material terms, then class is likely to be a major determinant of welfare; but the association is not a simple one. Although class and status are formally discrete concepts, status clearly depends on economic circumstances, and the concept of 'class' is overlaid with aspects of roles and status which are not wholly economic. The idea of 'social class', or socio-economic status, is a fusion of the two ideas.

Class, status, and power are interrelated. Class implies power in economic relationships, to the extent that money gives some people control over their lives and the lives of others. A person's status carries a degree of influence, or power in social relationships. There is a constant interaction between the different factors. Education and occupation affect life-style and expectations; people can use power or status to improve their economic position. Although the associations are not straightforward, there is a tendency towards inequality; the structure of social relationships leads to a reinforcement of advantage or disadvantage. Poverty implies lack of power, low status and a limited life-style.

In a number of respects, people in higher social classes seem to benefit more from public and social services than lower classes do, a fact which seems to support the view that society is organized for the benefit of those whose power is greatest. The welfare state, Pen writes,

> is often compared to Santa Claus, and that comparison is usually drawn by those who object to presents for poor people. But in fact the Welfare State resembles Santa Claus because he gives more to rich children than to poor ones.
>
> (Pen 1974: 370)

Le Grand notes that transport subsidies are greater for people who live at a greater distance from city centres, who tend to be richer (Le Grand 1982). Housing subsidies for owner-occupiers are greater than those for tenants. In education, middle-class families are more likely to stay in education above the age of 16, and in particular to occupy places in higher education in universities and polytechnics.

An illustration of the process is provided by the inequalities in treatment offered by the National Health Service. The Black Report shows that people in lower social classes are more likely to suffer from ill health, but that they nevertheless receive less help from the service (DHSS 1980). Part of the failure of treatment may be due to class discrimination – middle-class doctors prefer to work in congenial, middle-class environments, and perhaps tend to offer a better service to people who are able to articulate their problems in a language they share. But much disadvantage arises without conscious discrimination. It can be argued that there are subcultural differences: working-class patients may have lower expectations, and may be more inclined to defer to high-status professionals, than middle-class people are. There are also differences which stem from economic circumstances. Working-class people face greater costs in visiting the doctor. They have more difficulties in transport, less access to telephones, and are less free to take time off work without losing money for doing so. These points help to demonstrate why the idea of 'socio-economic status' is useful; it is a predictor of disadvantage, and as such it identifies groups of people with similar interests.

However, there are grounds for caution before concluding that this is evidence of the use of power by those who are relatively advantaged. If society is unequal to begin with, then any policy which fails to address the problems of inequality is at least as likely, or more likely, to favour higher social classes as lower ones. The criticism of the educational or health services is not so much that they have maintained the structure of society, as that they have failed to change it. There is an implicit assumption in this argument that education or health ought to lead to greater equality – a view which not everyone would share. Inequalities in provision can be seen, not as a result of policy which deliberately maintains an unequal society, but as a case where policy has simply not attempted to redress the sources of inequality which already exist. This reflects on the arguments on 'power' considered up to now. If we are referring to the workings of a system rather than the actions of specific groups, it is arguable whether we need to refer to 'power' at all to explain the advantages gained by people who are already privileged.

IX

Inequality

Summary: *Welfare is closely linked to command over resources, but resources are unequally distributed in society. Despite accusations to the contrary, the social services are redistributive to some extent, but there are problems in devising strategies for further redistribution. Selective policies, concentrating resources on the poor, may be divisive, but universal policies may fail adequately to redress inequalities.*

The distribution of resources in Britain is far from equal. Resources are normally considered as *income*, which is a *flow* of resources, or *wealth*, which is a *stock*. *The Economist*, in 1966, published figures suggesting that 7 per cent of the people in Britain owned 84 per cent of the nation's wealth. But this was based on investments, which is not the most appropriate measure of welfare. The Inland Revenue, concentrating on marketable wealth – that is, wealth that can be sold – suggest that the top 10 per cent of the population own 54 per cent of wealth (Central Statistical Office [CSO] 1986: 92). This is a more useful statistic, because 'marketable' wealth is more likely to include goods which will improve a person's life-style than investments are. Having said this, the figures are still fairly remote from 'welfare interests'. The measurement of wealth leaves much to be desired – Polanyi and Wood note undervaluation of popular assets like cars, no allowances for age differentials, difficulties in establishing just how much wealth there is, and some silly results – like the assertion that large numbers of people own nothing at all (Polanyi and Wood 1974). There is substantial uncertainty about just what should be included as wealth. On one hand, many households 'own' their own homes. The main share of the equity may be mortgaged to a building society or a bank, but the household has exclusive use, and it is this use which matters for the household's life-style. By contrast, many people 'own' pension rights, but they cannot do much with them;

the rights only have a significant value for them when they retire. When pension rights are included, the share of the top 10 per cent of households falls to 35 per cent of wealth (CSO 1986: 92), which is still unequal, but very much less unequal than before.

From the point of view of welfare, the question of ownership is of much less interest than the question of use. A family which owns its house has an accumulating capital asset, but it cannot realistically hope to sell it and live off the proceeds. A council tenant may well make a similar use of a house to an owner-occupier. There are possibly advantages in owner-occupation – like the ability to improve one's circumstances, to develop the property, and to leave capital to one's children – but it is questionable whether a person's wealth, measured by the capital value of assets, is a very good guide to welfare. Take the example of two elderly women, Ethel and Doris, widowed and living on their own. Ethel owns her own house, which is worth £15,000; Doris rents her house from the council, and has the rent paid by Housing Benefit because she is on a low income. Ethel cannot afford repairs, cannot manage the stairs, and cannot afford to move to a bungalow or ground-floor flat because they are too costly in her area. On paper, Ethel is far wealthier, but she can do little about it, and Doris, whose house is maintained by the council, seems to be in a preferable position.

The illustration can be extended further. Suppose that Doris's wedding ring is worth £50, and Ethel's is valued at £1,000. Doris has a fridge and a washing machine worth £200; Ethel does not. Their total other wealth is £500 each. Ethel's wealth, even disregarding housing, is double Doris's. There is nothing to stop Ethel selling her ring, and buying goods with it, but it is highly unlikely that she would. Other things being equal, Doris has more material comforts than Ethel, and it does not seem exaggerated to say that her welfare is greater.

Inequality of income is sometimes a more useful indicator of welfare, because people often have some choice about what to do with it which they do not have with their wealth. Inequalities in income are less pronounced than inequalities of wealth: the top 20 per cent of households have 40 per cent of income after tax and benefits, while the bottom 20 per cent have only 6.7 per cent (Byrne 1987: 36). These figures do not necessarily mean that there is a

Table 9.1 *Inequality during working life: an illustration*

Person	Age	Income	% total income
1	20	£ 5,000	5.3
2	24	£ 6,000	6.3
3	28	£ 7,000	7.4
4	32	£ 8,000	8.4
5	36	£ 9,000	9.5
6	40	£10,000	10.5
7	44	£11,000	11.5
8	48	£12,000	12.6
9	52	£13,000	13.6
10	56	£14,000	16.8

simple division between 'haves' and 'have nots'; people's circumstances tend to change over the life-cycle. For example, many people feel that a person of 35 should earn more than a person of 18, and that people of 18 are not at a disadvantage when they earn less now, because their income will increase later. This factor alone could create a very unequal distribution of income. To take a simple illustration, imagine the distribution between ten people shown in Table 9.1. The same kind of progression over the life-cycle creates many real problems. The main responsibilities for child care fall earlier in the age distribution, when there are lower incomes and fewer accumulated resources. The interruption of women's earnings means that families with young children in particular tend to have lower incomes. The effect is to create large disparities. These points can be seen in figure 9.1.

This helps to explain the source of inequality of incomes, and quite apart from the simple difference in income between classes it implies something about the likely differences in their life style and expectations.

But there are, in addition, inequalities between occupational groups and social classes. Manual wages tend to fall in later years, and non-manual wages to increase; non-manual occupations are much more likely to have an occupational pension when income falls on retirement. Over time, inequalities in income become reflected in differences in material circumstances, because people are able to buy

Figure 9.1 The effects of taxes and benefits, by selected life-cycle category of
households, United Kingdom, 1983

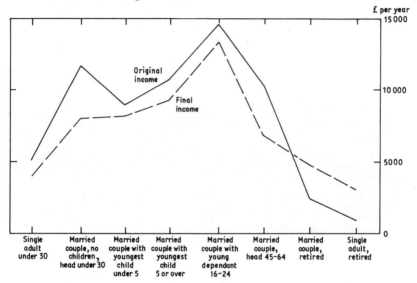

Source: CSO 1986: 91.

the things which make their lives better. People who are 'poor' –
lacking in resources – tend, for obvious reasons, to be those who fall
at the lower extremes of the income distribution.

Income, like wealth, is at best an indicator – a guide to the position
a person is likely to occupy. The real issue is not so much income as
command over resources, which is much more difficult to assess. It is
arguable whether figures based on individuals are the most appropriate to use. Many people can draw on other people's resources – a
husband or wife from each other, children from parents, elderly
people from adult children. Most households with low incomes
contain few people: many of them are pensioners. Households with
higher incomes tend to have more people in them. This means that
each individual may well have access to resources in a way that is
more equal than it first appears. Statistics for households may, then,
in some respects be more appropriate than figures for the whole
population. But feminist researches have shown that the distribution

Table 9.2 *An index of deprivation*

	Described as essential (%)	Unable to afford (%)
Heating	97	6
Indoor toilet	96	1
Damp-free home	96	8
Bath	94	2
Beds for everyone	94	1
Public transport	88	3
Warm waterproof coat	87	7
3 meals a day for children	82	4
Self-contained accommodation	79	3
2 pairs of all-weather shoes	78	11
Enough bedrooms for children	77	10
Refrigerator	77	1
Toys for children	71	3
Carpets	70	2
Celebrations on special occasions like Xmas	69	4
Roast joint or equivalent once a week	67	7
Washing machine	67	5

Source: Mack and Lansley 1985: 54, 89.

of income within families may be very unequal – women may be deprived even though the household income appears to be adequate (Pahl 1985). It is difficult, in cases of this type, to judge welfare adequately either from income or from wealth.

The deficiencies of these approaches emphasize the need to measure deprivation more directly. Townsend devises a 'deprivation index' to measure the effects of poverty. It includes factors like whether people have had a holiday, outings or entertainments, and whether they have had fresh meat or cooked breakfasts (Townsend 1979: 248–62). The index shows a consistent (if limited) relationship to low income. One of the great advantages of this approach is that, unlike a crude measure of income or wealth, it tells us the things we really want to know about people – how their command over resources affects their life-style. It is not a definition of poverty but a description of the ways in which people in our society can be considered deprived in relation to common expectations. Mack and Lansley (1982) have developed the technique further, outlining the gap between the items which people think essential and what poor people are actually able to afford (Table 9.2).

Table 9.2, they note, probably underestimates the lack of material goods. Some people may pretend to have items they don't have, because they don't want to be seen as inadequate or neglecting children. They may have low expectations, for example of what constitutes 'heating'. Most important, people may say they have 'chosen' not to have items which in fact they can't afford (*ibid.*: 105).

The people who lack essentials are not in general the same as those in 'social class V', the class of unskilled manual workers, even though those who have been in this class may be more likely to become poor through casual or intermittent employment. However, Mack and Lansley's research shows that they fall, fairly clearly, into the lowest income brackets (*ibid.*: 107–8). Poor people might be said to form a distinct class of their own, or perhaps an 'underclass'. They tend to share a common economic position; they are non-employed, financially dependent, and have low income and wealth.

POVERTY, INEQUALITY, AND THE SOCIAL SERVICES

There are three main approaches to poverty. One is to increase the total wealth available, in order to improve the living standards of the poor along with the rest of the population. Joseph and Sumption argue, 'You cannot make the poor richer by making the rich poorer, only by making everybody richer, including the rich' (Joseph and Sumption 1979: 22). The basic objection to this argument comes from those who see poverty as a relative concept. Any absolute increase in living standards is self-defeating: as wealth increases, so the basic definition of poverty shifts, and people continue to be deprived when compared with others. This is an important argument, because it tells us that poverty cannot be defeated in this way, though we should not conclude from this that increases in absolute standards do not matter; damp housing and lack of heat create health problems, and it is still better for a person's welfare to be poor in a dry, warm house than a cold, damp one.

The second approach is to redistribute resources directly from rich to poor. Crosland acknowledges, 'we have now reached the point where further redistribution would make little difference to the standard of living of the masses: to make the rich less rich would not make the poor significantly less poor' (Crosland 1956: 190). The simple truth of this should be clear from the fact that there are over nine and a quarter million pensioners. Each £1 on the pension costs nearly £500 million a year. But this is not an argument for failing to redistribute resources. Crosland argues that inequalities should be reduced, to make society more fair, to prevent the concentrations of power which accompany the accumulation of great wealth, and to help break down the class system (*ibid.*, Ch. 9). There is probably still a case, on this basis, to transfer resources directly from the richest person to the poorest person. Even so, it is important to realize that many of those who would be affected by redistribution of this kind are not 'rich'. Many households with two earners fall into the top 10 per cent of the income distribution, and the top third includes many people on average earnings – a fact which is less surprising when one remembers that nearly three households in ten are pensioners. Redistribution would not be painless.

Tawney argues that there is a value in redistributing the resources available. The point, he writes,

is not the division of the nation's income into eleven million fragments, to be distributed, without further ado, like a cake at a school treat, among its eleven million families. It is, on the contrary, the pooling of its surplus resources by means of taxation, and the use of the funds thus obtained to make accessible to all, irrespective of their income, occupation or social position, the conditions of civilisation which, in the absence of such measures, can only be enjoyed by the rich.

(Tawney 1931: 122)

The third approach is, then, to seek to raise the standards of the poorest by providing a basis of services available to everyone. The pooling of resources by the state may make the provision of certain goods and services more effectively than the private market, and the poor, as those most disadvantaged in the private market, should be the main gainers.

Table 9.3 *The redistribution of income through taxes and benefits, 1983*

	Quintile groups of households, ranked by original income				
	Bottom fifth	Next fifth	Middle fifth	Next fifth	Top fifth
Average initial income per household (£s)	120	2,580	6,880	10,570	18,640
plus					
Benefits in cash:					
Age-related	1,420	1,280	390	210	150
Child-related	130	140	300	310	260
Income-related	1,240	540	280	140	130
Other cash benefits	230	300	130	90	60
Total benefits in cash	3,020	2,260	1,100	750	600
Benefits in kind:					
Education	360	370	650	710	780
National Health Service	750	700	660	620	620
Housing subsidy	130	80	70	50	20
Other allocated benefits	100	100	90	100	140
less					
Income tax and national insurance	10	410	1,410	2,340	4,510
Indirect taxes	850	1,270	1,860	2,280	3,380
Final income	3,630	4,400	6,190	8,160	12,920
Average no. of people per household:					
Adults	1.5	1.7	2.0	2.2	2.6
Children	0.4	0.4	0.9	0.9	0.7
Total	1.9	2.1	2.9	3.1	3.3
Final income per capita	1,910	2,100	2,130	2,630	3,920

Source: CSO 1986.

The redistributive effects of social services are difficult to assess with any precision, because the indicators that are used – income and expenditure – give only a rough idea of the quality of life or the total command over resources a person has (Table 9.3). Subject to this reservation, they do seem to have a substantial impact on inequality.

It is arguable just how great the reduction in inequality is, because household composition clearly makes a large difference; there is no consideration of distribution within households, and the crude indication of income 'per capita' takes no account of the difference between adults and children. O'Higgins argues that when household data are adjusted for equivalence, the figures are substantially more egalitarian than they appear at first. The NHS and education are used equally by individuals at different income levels, and social security tends to increase equality overall (O'Higgins 1985). Education and child-related cash benefits may seem to offer more to those with higher incomes, but even on the crude figures presented here they are worth more proportionately to the poorest fifth than the richest fifth. And the NHS, despite what was said in the previous chapter, has a moderately progressive effect; this is mainly because of the cost of medical care for the elderly.

The main weaknesses in these observations lie in the reservations made earlier: income is only one measure of command over resources, and it may not be completely reliable; and the crude vertical measure of inequality gives an imperfect understanding of the kinds of social division that are present. In particular, the concentration of elderly people in the lowest income brackets means that this table represents a distribution of income at a particular moment in time; it may be more appropriate to consider the distribution of income over the life-cycle.

UNIVERSAL AND SELECTIVE SOCIAL BENEFITS

The effect of social services in distributing resources to people who already have high incomes has attracted considerable comment, and forms a major element in the debate between *selective* and *universal* services. A selective benefit is one which gives help directly to those most in need. On the face of it, this is exactly what is required in order to redistribute resources – transferring them from richest to poorest. And yet egalitarians have tended to oppose selectivity, for the following reasons.

The first objection to selectivity is the way in which it is done. In order to find out just who is poor or in need, some test is required. So, the form for Supplementary Benefit claimants asked:

'Why did you leave your job?'

'Are you married, or living with someone as if you are married to them?'

'Do you (or your partner or children who live with you) have any other money coming in apart from benefits? (such as money from a court order, maintenance, pensions from work or a retainer from boarders).'

This is often seen as a special problem of means-testing, but other benefits which have tests of need can be just as searching. Claimants for Attendance Allowance, for example, may have to establish that they are unable to wash themselves or use a toilet without someone else's help. The questions which are asked in means tests are widely believed to generate fear and suspicion, though my own observation would be that confusion is more common. Tests of this sort are necessarily intrusive, and there tends to be a presupposition that the claimant is likely to be dishonest.

Second, tests of means or needs have to make a distinction between those who are eligible and those who are not. There is a problem of equity; some people will receive help while others whose circumstances are very slightly different will not. But there is another issue as well: as people's circumstances improve, it is necessary to withdraw benefits from them. The problem is most apparent for means-tested benefits. When the loss of benefits is added to tax and national insurance contributions one may be worse off after an increase in earnings. This problem has become known as the 'poverty trap'. However, it is not only a problem of means-testing. Mobility Allowance is refused to people who can walk with an artificial limb, which is a discouragement to rehabilitation; Attendance Allowance is not available to those who can cope by themselves. For people in need, there is a disincentive to improve their circumstances.

Third, the process of testing is expensive, administratively burdensome, and time-consuming. In order to be sensitive to individual needs, schemes become more and more detailed: Supplementary Benefit (which has now been renamed 'Income Support') has more than 16,000 paragraphs of rules. The sheer complexity of the system made it inefficient; the officials did not know the rules, claimants did not know what to claim, and people in need were missed (see PSI 1984). But this is not necessarily intrinsic to selectivity. The basic problem with Supplementary Benefit was that the benefits were not high enough, which made it necessary to add a whole range of additional qualifications and payments to the basic structure. This could reasonably have been overcome, in large part, by the relatively simple device of raising the benefit; instead, the government chose to simplify the system by reducing the levels of benefit available to many claimants, causing great hardship.

Fourth, and most fundamentally, selectivity is believed to be stigmatizing. In part, this happens because selective services label claimants – marking them out as unemployed, disabled, single parents, and so on. The problem is less that the label itself is derogatory, than that it identifies a group which is socially rejected. But the objections to selectivity run deeper than this. Townsend argues that it

> fosters hierarchical relationships of superiority and inferiority in society, diminishes rather than enhances the status of the poor, and has the effect of widening rather than reducing social inequalities. Far from sensitively discriminating different kinds of needs it lumps the unemployed, sick, widowed, aged and others into one undifferentiated and inevitably stigmatised category.
> (Townsend 1976: 126)

Reddin accepts that selectivity has in theory a potential to reduce inequality, but sees the problems as insurmountable (Reddin 1970). The burden of proof, he argues, lies with those who favour selectivity to show that its fundamental problems can be overcome.

The main alternative to selectivity is universality. Universality implies, in theory, that services are available to all – a central principle of 'the welfare state'. In practice, universal services – like

Child Benefit or comprehensive education – are available not to
everyone but to everyone in a general category, like children or old
people. This causes some confusion when trying to decide whether
services for the 'disabled' are universal or selective. The emphasis has
to fall on the breadth of the category. The main advantage of
universality seems to be that it helps to conceal socially disadvantaged
groups; the wider the category, the less obvious the groups in
greatest need become. Child Benefit, for example, helps poor
families by giving them a flat-rate benefit, which is proportionately a
greater part of their income than it is of those with higher incomes,
but it does not single them out in the process.

Universal benefits, the Laroque Report suggests, 'contribute to a
nation's sense of community and interdependence – to national
solidarity' (ILO 1984: 23). Putting this less idealistically, the fact that
rich people as well as poor people use the services means that the
service is less likely to be treated as a second-class one; they will have
an interest in improving the quality of the service, and, Le Grand
argues, it will be less vulnerable politically than a service directed at
an unpopular, stigmatized group (Le Grand 1984).

Perhaps most important, universality implies equality of status
among recipients:

> One fundamental historical reason for the adoption of this
> principle was the aim of making services available and accessible to
> the whole population in such ways as would not involve users in any
> humiliating loss of status, dignity or self-respect. . . . If these
> services were not provided by everybody for everybody they would
> either not be available at all, or only for those who could afford
> them, and for others on such terms as would involve the infliction
> of a sense of inferiority and stigma.
>
> (Titmuss 1968: 129)

The idea that services are provided 'by everybody for everybody' is
eyewash, but the principle is clear enough.

However, there are problems with universality. In the first place, it
is costly. Pen compares the idea of some universal measures to 'filling
the sky with shot to hit a single duck' (Pen 1974: 377). Poverty is
perhaps a little more prevalent than this suggests, but the point is a
valid one: most resources will be applied to people in no special need.

This is evident from Table 9.3; even if the distribution of resources is progressive, most of the spending goes to people who are not in the bottom 20 per cent of income groups.

This has important implications for supporters of universality who would also like to see greater substantive equality. The route to greater equality is through more efficient redistribution – which implies greater selectivity. Le Grand argues that the 'universal' health service has failed to equalize the position of the poor precisely because it is committed to help everyone (Le Grand 1982). This has made it in practice of greatest benefit to the middle classes. And the education service, because it provides for all without discriminating in favour of those who are poorest, substantially benefits those on higher incomes. In effect, universality creates the conditions in which inequality flourishes. He concludes that the 'strategy of equality' through increasing public expenditure and universal services, has failed. Several arguments can be made against this case. The services have not failed to help the poor; they have helped them less, perhaps, than might have been looked for, but they still provide real and important benefits for those unable to afford them. The effect of most benefits is to create greater equality to some degree, when their role in proportion to the income of poor households is considered. As O'Higgins argues, the provision of universal benefits helps to create equality, if not of equivalent income from the services, of access, provision, and so of social security, in its widest sense – the reassurance provided by social protection (O'Higgins 1987). And if universal benefits are financed by progressive taxation, the overall effect will still be progressive. The principal argument against universality is not that it has not been worthwhile, but that the problems might have been better approached in some other way – if only we can work out what the other way should be.

X

Equality

Summary: *Equality means the removal of disadvantage. Egalitarian policies may aim for equal treatment, without prejudice or stigma; equal opportunity, the means to achieve socially desired ends; and equality of result, in which disadvantages are removed altogether. The idea of 'positive discrimination' seems to go beyond equality, by seeking to compensate for disadvantage in society as a whole by favourable treatment in a selected area. This can create conflicts between different ideas of equality.*

The idea of 'inequality' implies that there is something about a person which gives that person an advantage, or creates disadvantage, relative to others. One common classification distinguishes *vertical inequality* from *horizontal inequality*. Vertical inequality is a comparison between people with basically similar needs; it contrasts rich and poor, or people with different classes or statuses. Horizontal inequality compares people in different positions – like couples with children against couples without. This distinction is not a very clear one, because there are some groups (like women, blacks, disabled, and old people) who are likely to have inferior income and status, and it is not obvious how far this should be taken as 'vertical' or 'horizontal'.

Rae argues that comparisons are made not only between individuals but also between *blocs* and *segments* of society (Rae 1981). 'Bloc regarding' inequality is applied between subgroups; it describes the disadvantage of one group of people relative to another. Many important issues in social policy, like race, sex, or policy for the inner cities, are bloc-regarding. The idea of 'segment regarding' inequality is more difficult, because it is unfamiliar. The concept makes comparisons within subgroups of society, not between them: for example, inequality of women compared to other women, inequality within a region, inequality between pensioners. An example of a

study which concentrates on a segment is entitled *Born to Fail*
(Wedge and Prosser 1973) which shows the accumulated disadvantages of some children relative to others. It is based on a study of
over 10,000 eleven-year-old children. The most disadvantaged
children were those living in either large or single-parent families
with low income and bad housing. The vast majority were working
class. These children lacked basic amenities in the home and were
likely to share beds. They were shorter than other children, liable to
more absence from ill health, more subject to accidents, more likely
to suffer impairment of vision, hearing, or speech, to be treated as
'maladjusted', to be of low educational ability, and to be in special
education. They were more than ten times likely than others to be
in care before the age of 11 (*ibid.*: 26). Even if this disadvantage is
not maintained in later life (and Brown and Madge's study *Despite
the Welfare State* [1982] suggests, perhaps surprisingly, that in most
cases it is not), the disadvantage experienced in childhood is a
legitimate cause of concern in itself.

The aim of policies for equality is to remove the disadvantages
which people experience in society. 'Equality' is not, as some critics
would have it, 'sameness'; people are dissimilar in many ways, but
this is not the same as saying that they are unequal. Some critics of
egalitarianism misunderstand this position. L.P. Hartley, for example, wrote a novel called *Facial Justice* (1960) in which beautiful
people are made to have cosmetic surgery to make them uglier, and
ugly people are made less ugly. This is his way of saying that some
inequalities are 'natural', and desirable; the novel has been cited
with approval by Schoek (1969) and by Sir Keith Joseph. But the
parable misses the point; it is arguing against a position that no-one
holds. Where disadvantage arises as a result of differences, like race
or sex, the aim of egalitarian policies is to change the relationships –
not necessarily to eliminate the differences themselves. Tawney's
classic work *Equality* makes the point forcefully. What writers on
equality are emphasizing, he states,

> is not equality of capacity or attainment, but of circumstances,
> institutions and manner of life. The inequality which they de-
> plore is not inequality of personal gifts, but of the social and
> economic environment. They are concerned, not with a biological

phenomenon, but with a spiritual relation and the conduct to be
based on it. Their view, in short, is that because men are men, social
institutions – property rights, and the organisation of industry,
and the system of public health and education – should be
planned, as far as possible, to emphasise and strengthen, not the
class differences which divide, but the common humanity which
unites, them.

(Tawney 1931: 48–9)

A much more subtle and effective critique of egalitarianism is made
by Charvet (1983). He argues that man is social; activity in society
means that people adopt roles; and roles necessarily mean differen-
tiation, and varied degrees of respect. Disadvantage, it follows, is the
normal pattern of society. The idea of 'equality', he suggests, tries to
divorce people from a social context; it is, therefore, basically
unrealistic. The aim of achieving greater equality is an attempt to
import a normative principle into conditions which may frustrate all
the efforts of reformers to correct them. Tawney's case is that there is
no moral reason why one should have to accept things as they are,
and the case for greater equality is that we should try to do what is
right – even if the attempt is unsuccessful:

> What matters to the health of society is the direction towards which
> its face is set, and to suggest that it is immaterial in which direction
> it moves, because, whatever the direction, the goal must always
> elude it, is not scientific, but irrational. It is like using the
> impossibility of absolute cleanliness as an excuse for rolling in a
> manure heap, or denying the importance of honesty because
> no-one can be wholly honest.

(*ibid.*: 56)

The strength of this argument depends on to what extent greater
equality is seen as being morally desirable.

Egalitarian policies are commonly framed in three ways. There is
the prevention of disadvantage in access to services, or *equal treatment*.
There is the removal of disadvantage in competition with others,
which is *equality of opportunity*. And there is the complete removal of
disadvantage in practice – *equality of result*. This is not an exhaustive
classification (see Rae 1981), but it represents some of the main
features of egalitarianism in an applied context.

The argument for equality of treatment is an argument for treatment without favour, without prejudice. This could mean, Dworkin writes, neutrality between people; but it can also be extended, he suggests, to treatment within a particular framework of values (Dworkin 1985: 192). Titmuss, for example, argues:

> There should be no sense of inferiority, pauperism, shame or stigma in the use of a publicly provided service: no attribution that one was being or becoming a "public burden". Hence the emphasis on the social rights of all citizens to use or not to use as responsible people the services made available by the community.
>
> (Titmuss 1968: 129)

Dworkin tries to distinguish equal treatment from treatment as an equal. Equal treatment is 'the right to an equal distribution of some opportunity or resource or burden', or the right to be treated identically in certain matters; treatment as an equal is the right 'to be treated with the same respect and concern as anyone else' (Dworkin 1978: 227). This distinction is based in a confusion of ideas; the idea of equal treatment is not used in the way he suggests. As Benn and Peters comment, 'we should not wish rheumatic patients to be treated like diabetics' (Benn and Peters 1959: 108). When equal treatment is identified as treatment without disadvantage, Dworkin's distinction collapses.

The second main form of equality is equality of opportunity. The idea is potentially ambiguous. Rae points out that it can be *prospect regarding*, implying that people are able to participate on the same terms in a contest that anyone could win, or *means regarding*, which implies that they have equal means to achieve the end (Rae 1981). In the former sense, equality of opportunity is simply equivalent to equal treatment; in the latter, Schaar writes, 'the formula can be used to express the fundamental proposition that no member of the community should be denied the basic conditions necessary for the fullest participation in public life' (Schaar 1971: 146). Equality of opportunity has been an influential concept in the context of educational policy (see Silver 1973). The 'tripartite' system of education set up in 1944, of grammar, secondary modern, and technical schools, was intended to give its pupils 'parity of esteem' – a form of equal treatment. It soon became apparent, though, that the system did not offer any genuine equality, and that the opportunities of working-class children in particular were severely circumscribed. In competition with middle-class children, the middle classes were far more likely to achieve better results, to go on to higher education, and to emerge in consequence in better jobs. The education system was therefore seen by egalitarians as a primary source of social inequality (see Tawney 1931; Crosland 1956). The introduction of comprehensive education – the unification of the tripartite system, and the removal of selection at the age of 11 – was intended to remove much of this problem, as was the expansion of the universities and the development of the polytechnics.

The disadvantages faced by working-class children were, however, only partly caused by the inequalities of the school system – in consequence of which, Szamuely argues, the reforms actually reduced the opportunities of the brightest working-class children to escape from disadvantaged circumstances (Szamuely 1971). Reports in the 1950s and 1960s pointed to disadvantage arising through pressure to leave school, the basis of arguments for the raising of the school leaving age; and through the lack of qualifications obtained by most school leavers, which led to the introduction of CSE examinations. These measures represent a movement towards equality of opportunity, in so far as they attempted to equalize the conditions under which people were competing. It is worth pointing out that the stress on opportunity may, however, have had negative effects. The emphasis has fallen on equality in educational competition, rather than on educational standards as a precondition for equality of opportunity in society; educational testing has in consequence been mainly concentrated on comparison with other pupils, rather than the achievement of basic levels of competence.

The aim of equality of opportunity is in any case a limited one. Tawney refers to the prospect of a thousand donkeys 'induced to sweat by the prospect of a carrot that could only be eaten by one' (Tawney 1931: 111). We might think of equality of opportunity more accurately as a game of musical chairs: there are places for many people, but by no means enough, and someone has to lose. There are also fears that the existence of inequality perpetuates the disadvantages of the lower-status groups. From the point of view of welfare, this may not be acceptable. If we want to establish minimum standards relative to the whole population, it is necessary to look at greater equality not only of opportunity but also of result.

Tony Crosland, who is often represented as a leading advocate of equality of opportunity, in fact criticized the concept forcefully. In Britain, he argued:

> equality of opportunity and social mobility . . . are not enough. They need . . . to be combined with measures . . . to equalise the distribution of rewards and privileges so as to diminish the degree of class stratification, the injustice of large inequalities, and the collective discontents which come from too great a dispersion of rewards.
>
> (Crosland 1956: 237)

Egalitarian policies may, consequently, aim for equality of result as a logical extension of the desire to limit disadvantage in society. This may be pursued through a number of strategies. Rae outlines four (Rae 1981, Ch. 6). The first is *maximin*, maximizing the minimum. This implies the raising of minimum standards – standards of housing, levels of income, levels of education and health care. This could be done either through selective or universal policies. The second is to address the *ratio* of inequality, increasing the resources of those who are worst off relative to those who are best off. I pointed out in the last chapter that education and child-related benefits have this effect, even though they distribute more to households on higher incomes. Third, equality may aim for the *least difference*, reducing the range of inequality. Education does not have this effect; age-related benefits do. The fourth is *minimax*, or reducing the advantage of those who are most privileged – private education which gives an advantage to some in competition for places in higher education or the job market, private health care which allows some people to be treated at the cost of delay to others, or the privileges associated with high incomes. Rae argues that each of these strategies leads to a greater degree of equality than the last. This is probably right in practice, though not in logic; any of these four approaches, taken to an extreme, would lead to equality of result.

However, the different approaches to equality – equality of treatment, of opportunity, and result – do represent a progressively extending commitment to intervention. Each is motivated by the same guiding principle – the desire to remove disadvantage – though they differ in the extent and scope to which they prevent or compensate for it.

POSITIVE DISCRIMINATION

The concept of 'positive discrimination' represents a major change in the focus of egalitarian policies. The term was introduced in the United Kingdom in the Plowden Report, *Children and Their Primary Schools* (DES 1967) – reflecting again, the concern for equality in educational policy. The report noted that schools in poor areas had low standards and were unable to cope with their problems. It argued for the creation of Educational Priority Areas (EPAs) to meet these needs. The EPA, based in the school, would seek to minimize educational disadvantage by providing the best services possible.

In practice, EPAs failed to live up to the report's expectations. In part, this is because the attempts to implement the committee's recommendations were half-hearted: only limited funds were made available, and local authorities were reluctant to forward schemes. But it also reflects inadequacies in the concept. The policy possibly exaggerated the potential of the education system to deal with poverty and social inequality. There was, besides, a central misconception in the report about the distribution of disadvantage. The idea of EPAs assumed a geographical concentration of poor children. Although it was true that these areas had a higher proportion of poor children than others, poverty was far more widespread. Most of the people in EPAs were not poor, and, more important most poor people were not in EPAs. Only two deprived children in five were covered (Barnes and Lucas 1975).

The EPA experiment is significant in two ways. First, by emphasizing a localized, geographical approach, the Plowden Report marked the beginnings of a shift in policy from person-regarding to bloc-regarding equality – that is, from individuals to groups. This way of thinking about the issues was to become a major part of the Urban Programme. Second, the report argued:

There should be equality of opportunity for all, but . . . children in some districts will only get the same opportunity as those who live elsewhere if they have unusually generous treatment. . . . We ask for 'positive discrimination' in favour of such schools and the children in them, going well beyond an attempt to equalise resources.

(DES 1967: 151)

The point of positive discrimination is not simply that schools in poor areas should receive more funds than other schools, or even that they should be brought up to the level of others; this would remove disadvantage in one respect without affecting it in others. The report wanted to make these schools *better* than others, to help make up for the disadvantages that children experience outside the schools as well as those they suffer in them.

This concept has been the source of great confusion. Titmuss refers to the challenge of 'positively discriminating on a territorial "group of rights" basis in favour of the poor, the handicapped, the deprived, the coloured, the homeless and the social casualties of our society' (Titmuss 1968: 134) when it is clear that he is not talking about positive discrimination at all. It is not positive discrimination to create jobs for unemployed people, to provide aids for the handicapped, to give money to poor people; it is simple egalitarianism. Positive discrimination implies that people are first treated equally – and then treated better.

If positive discrimination is egalitarian, it is because it compensates people in one sector for disadvantage in another, or because it makes up for past disadvantage. It may achieve equality of result overall, but it does so at the expense of equal treatment and equal opportunity. The argument is that inequality in one respect may lead to greater equality in others. An example of this is the use of 'affirmative action' in the United States to allow blacks access to medical school. This puts people who are not black at a disadvantage. The policy is hotly contested: the Bakke case – a legal action taken by a white student excluded in favour of a black student with inferior qualifications – illustrates the point (see Dworkin 1985, Chs. 14 and 15).

One justification is that blacks have been disadvantaged in the educational process previously, and their advancement at this stage makes up for prior disadvantage. Against this, it can be argued that people who have been disadvantaged educationally may not be competent at a job which requires high qualifications. (This is contestable in the field of medicine. The level of qualifications required is more a reflection of the demand for places than of the qualities necessary for the job). A further justification is that blacks are not being adequately provided with medical care, and more qualified blacks will provide this. But the root of the disadvantage is not necessarily racial. Blacks do not receive inferior medical care because it is given by white doctors; another view of the problem is that they are more likely to be poor, and poor people – both black and white – receive inferior care. There is no evidence, Bowie and Simon note, that black doctors are more likely to help black patients (Bowie and Simon 1977: 267).

The problem with affirmative action is that discrimination in favour of some groups is equivalent to discrimination against others. Concepts of advantage and disadvantage are relative; if one person is given an advantage in a competition, it is at the expense of someone else. In the United States, blacks and Hispanics tend to be relatively disadvantaged in education, Jews and Japanese students are relatively more successful. Inegalitarian policies which discriminate in favour of blacks discriminate against Jews, Japanese, *and* Hispanics. If race is a criterion for positive discrimination, it must also be seen as a criterion for negative discrimination; they are two sides of the same coin. (I have this argument from Laurence Lustgarten.) Dworkin argues forcefully that there is a qualitative difference between the use of race as a criterion for selection, and disadvantage which arises through prejudice and contempt:

> The United States will continue to be pervaded by racial divisions as long as the most lucrative, satisfying and important careers remain mainly the prerogative of the white race, while others feel themselves systematically excluded from a professional and social elite.
>
> (Dworkin 1985: 284)

The issue of affirmative action, Rae argues, brings different concepts of equality into conflict. It opposes equality of opportunity, the opportunity to enter college on equal terms, with equality of results. It is means regarding, attempting to give blacks the means to become equal, rather than prospect regarding, promoting a contest on equal terms. Third, affirmative action is bloc regarding, not person regarding; it overlooks individual disadvantage. It may favour a rich black student over a poor white one (Rae 1981: 81).

The main problem with positive discrimination is that it may disadvantage some people unfairly. This stems as much from the focus on blocs as from the idea of positive discrimination itself. The trouble with bloc-regarding approaches is the risk that, in concentrating on one relevant difference between people, they may overlook others. Rich women may gain at the expense of poor men, men in the inner city at the expense of women in outlying areas, or gifted black children at the expense of educationally deprived whites. The difficulty here seems to be not that such policies are egalitarian but that they are not egalitarian enough. The purpose of positive discrimination is to redress a balance; but the sources of inequality in society are complex. If positive discrimination is to be effective in dealing with disadvantage, it has to be done with a clearer understanding of the problems it faces.

The arguments for redistribution enshrined in egalitarian policies are fairly simple ones, even if the policies themselves are not. Because welfare services are redistributive, they can be a means to reduce inequality – and indeed, the effect of inequality on welfare is a major reason for seeking to reduce it. However, there is more than this to be considered. Some disadvantages may be legitimate. There are other values besides welfare which have to be considered – like rights, reward for merit, and property. The discussion of redistribution in relation to these values has centred mainly around the issue of 'social justice'.

XI

Social Justice

Summary: *Distributive justice involves distribution proportionate to certain criteria; the criteria could include need, rights, desert, work, and many others. There is a presumption of equality where there are no relevant distinguishing criteria, but the principle is not necessarily egalitarian.*

The concept of 'social justice' has attracted more attention in recent years than any other question in political theory. This interest is largely attributable to John Rawls's massive book, *A Theory of Justice* (1971). Rawls uses the idea of a 'social contract' to establish the basis of a 'just' society. From this contract, he argues, two main rules emerge. The first is that liberty is the most important rule of social justice, and a just society must preserve liberty. The second is that inequalities must be acceptable to everyone, as part of a fair system.

Rawls's theory is presented in a highly abstract form, and as Barry rightly comments, the book 'has hardly anything to say about social policy (a significantly low priority when one considers that for many working class people in industrial societies "fairness" is virtually entirely comprised in the provisions of the welfare state') (Barry 1973: 57). In his later work Rawls has attempted to remedy this deficiency by considering the nature of the goods that are to be distributed (Rawls 1982). He refers to certain 'primary goods', which are of particular importance for each individual; they include basic civil and political rights, income and wealth, and what he terms the 'social bases of self-respect'. Citizens have basic needs that must be met:

Citizens' needs are objective in a way that desires are not; that is, they express requirements of persons with certain highest-order interests who have a certain social role and status. If these

requirements are not met, persons cannot maintain their role or
status, or achieve their essential aims.

(ibid.: 172)

In a 'just' society, some differences in these goods would be
acceptable only if everyone (or at least the worst off person) is better
off as a result of them – which may happen if, for example, the
inequalities create incentives for people to work harder and increase
the wealth of society as a whole.

Rawls effectively equates the concept of 'justice' with a normative
theory of distribution. This seems to me to be a confusion about the
idea of 'justice'. The social contract is a device for determining
whether a policy can be said to be legitimate, which is to say, 'right'.
This is not the same as saying the policy is 'just'. Because justice is
itself a morally approved principle, we can say that an action which is
'just' is likely to be 'right' if it does not conflict with other principles.
But there are other principles. Rawls himself accepts there may be
some exception for special medical and health needs, but does not
explain his grounds for thinking so. The point is that other moral
imperatives may affect the distribution of resources besides 'justice'
alone. Justice is a much more limited concept than legitimacy,
related, as Rawls himself argues, to fairness.

Aristotle distinguished two main kinds of justice: *corrective* justice,
or justice in relation to punishment, or *distributive* justice, justice in
relation to resources (Thomson 1953). The guiding principle of
corrective justice is that the punishment would be proportionate to
the crime – which is why the committal of the child to long-term care
may seem 'unjust'. The principle of distributive justice is *equity*, a
distribution proportionate to accepted criteria, like status, merit,
contribution to society, or need. If, for example, merit is accepted as
a relevant criterion, then it is just for a person of greater merit to
receive greater resources.

David Miller, in his book on *Social Justice* (1976), gives examples of
three very different views of justice, which he selects because they
show in an extreme form what happens when justice is taken on
different criteria. David Hume, the eighteenth-century philosopher,
sees justice in terms of recognition of property rights. These rights
are based in present possession; rights of occupation; 'prescription',

or the process by which rights become accepted or established over
time; rights of accession (i.e. rules which govern the process of
acquiring property); and rights of succession (or transfer). Hume's
view is conservative, in the sense that his idea of justice acts to
preserve the current distribution of resources. Herbert Spencer, the
Victorian social theorist, bases a concept of justice in 'desert', which
he equates with contribution to society, measured by a person's
rewards in a free economic market. (Hayek argues, I think rightly,
that desert and contribution to society are not equivalent [Hayek
1984]. A person may deserve more for trying harder, but rewards for
contribution to society reflect results rather than effort.) Spencer's
model clearly relates to a particular view of society and private
enterprise. Kropotkin, a Russian anarchist, sees justice as based
exclusively in need. This model would – unlike the other two –
identify justice closely with redistribution for welfare.

Miller describes these as distinct theories of justice, which in a sense
they are. But they can also be seen as different applications of a
principle of proportion. Rights, desert, and need are different
criteria which can be seen as relevant in different circumstances.
Although the theorists Miller selects would reject the other
viewpoints, it would be quite possible to mix the criteria – to accept
that all of them are relevant in some respects – and in practice, this is
what we largely do. Furthermore, in practice the application of the
criteria will vary considerably, because rights, desert, and need are
socially defined. Walzer argues:

> In a world of particular cultures, competing conceptions of the
> good, scarce resources, elusive and expansive needs, there isn't
> going to be a single formula, universally applicable. There isn't
> going to be a single universally approved path that carries us from
> a notion like, say, 'fair shares' to a comprehensive list of the goods
> to which that notion applies. Fair shares of what?
>
> (Walzer 1984: 205)

The principle of justice is not necessarily 'egalitarian': a concept of
social justice based on need may imply substantial equality, but one
based on desert or traditional property rights could be expected to
lead to an unequal distribution. But the idea of proportionate
distribution helps to explain why justice is linked with equality – an

assumption which Rawls makes but, as Nozick comments, fails to make explicit (Nozick 1974: 160–4). The reason why inequalities must be justified is simply a demand for consistency; as Flew writes, 'If I claim I have a right, on some ground, then I necessarily concede, by the same claim, a corresponding right to everyone else who satisfies that same condition' (Flew 1981: 42). It would be inconsistent to argue for differing rights in cases where no relevant factors distinguished the people involved. A principle of proportionate distribution implies equal treatment in those cases where the people who are dealt with cannot otherwise be distinguished by relevant criteria. This is fundamental to the argument for equality.

JUSTICE AND PROPERTY

The idea of 'justice' is primarily related to social welfare in so far as it affects the distribution of resources. Nozick argues that justice should imply a protection of property rights (Nozick 1974). Any distribution produced by a process of legitimate transfers and acquisitions must itself be just, on a principle he calls 'historical'. Steiner objects that, for those being born into the society on these terms, this is a bit like joining a game of Monopoly after the properties have been sold (Steiner 1981).

A concept of justice which depended on the defence of property rights would limit redistribution substantially. In the simplest terms, redistribution would be theft. If you have two coats and I have one, would it be 'just' for me to take yours away? Brennan and Friedman argue, from a 'libertarian' perspective, that property stems from the work of an individual:

> The libertarian does not consider the world as a place in which bread falls from heaven, where the proper moral problem is one of dividing it, but as a place where individuals produce things of value – bake bread . . . and where each such thing thus appears not as common property, but as the property of a particular individual.
> (Brennan and Friedman 1981: 27)

Hayek is able to find no moral justification for 'social justice' at all (Hayek 1976). And Schoek argues that the idea is nothing more than envy – the envy of people who want the possessions of others (Schoek

1969). This is an extreme argument, but it is an important one if we are to understand the basis of 'social justice' in practice. What is the difference between theft and taxation to pay for welfare services? It would be easy to reply that people 'tacitly consent' to taxation, but they have probably had little or no choice in the matter.

There are at least six basic arguments. The first is that property rights are a matter, not of morally indisputable eternal truths, but of convention and tradition. (For example, it has not always been universally true that property is owned by individuals; in some societies, property rights have been held by families.) Taxation is as much a part of the conventions of our society as rights of possession are; there is a good argument to suggest that what people earn takes into account the amount they will have to pay in tax. Theft is illegitimate, by definition; taxation is, by the same kinds of social convention, legitimate, and so is not theft. This is more than a play with words; it refers to the view that what is 'legitimate' and what is not is based, not on moral certainties, but on practices which are generally accepted over time.

The second view is that property does not come from the efforts of individuals in the way Brennan and Friedman suggest, but from the conditions and patterns of work established in a particular society. Baking bread, or any other productive activity, would not happen as if the worker were living on a desert island; the ingredients are bought, the water is drawn by the efforts of others, the fuel is delivered, the oven is manufactured by others, the recipe has been learnt. It is, then, like all other activities, social; and the claim to own what is produced is also social.

Third, there is the opinion that it is property right, not the redistribution, which has to be justified. If resources should be distributed equally unless there are relevant differences, the onus falls on those who claim property to explain the basis of their continued possession.

Fourth, the view of Marx and others is that the distribution of ownership reflects not the individuals who have produced things of value, but exploitation by the few. Friedman suggests that there is a contradiction in the traditional Marxist position; it is not possible to argue both that people should keep what they earn and that people should receive according to need (Friedman 1962). In fact, the problem was recognized by Marx: in the *Critique of the Gotha Programme*, he took the position that the proceeds of labour should be seen as a 'total social product' (Marx 1875). From this, he argued, the resources necessary for industry had to be deducted, followed by the costs of administration, funding for 'the common satisfaction of needs, such as schools, health services etc.', and 'funds for those unable to work, etc., in short, for what is included under so-called official poor relief today'. It was only then that resources could be considered to be available for consumption by individuals (*ibid.*: 318–19). In other words, Marx is assuming the prior claim of society to resources from production. (Lenin subsequently worked out principles for redistribution which were a compromise between the two positions: this formed the basis for taxation and social security in the Soviet Union: see George and Manning 1980, Ch. 2.)

Fifth, it is possible to argue that the same rights which legitimate property ownership also legitimate redistribution. Weale begins from an emphasis on autonomy, or individual freedom (Weale 1983, Ch. 4). This depends in part on personal rights to protect people against the abuse of centralized power; it also demands some rights of consumption, or the enjoyment of goods. Property is some guarantee of both. By the same argument, though, people who have nothing to consume have a right to redistribution which will preserve their autonomy as individuals. This means that both property and welfare are essential for personal freedom.

Sixth, and possibly most important, is that the person in need has a claim which outweighs the property rights of the person in possession – in other words, that there is a conflict of principles.

'Justice' cannot be judged solely in terms of the person who benefits from it; it must also consider the person who has to pay. Amdur classifies three main categories of people who lose as a result of distributive justice (Amdur 1979). There are those who have committed an injustice. So, in the courts, if a person is injured through another person's fault, one person has to compensate the other. (This is a position which itself has led to frequent accusations of unfairness, because it means that a person who is able to demonstrate another's fault can receive help denied to others with identical needs. The main justification for the system – discontinued in New Zealand – is the desire to retain personal responsibility for compensation: see Cmnd 7054, 1978; Atiyah 1980). It is possible to extend this argument a little further and to argue that the higher social classes should compensate the lower classes for the 'injuries' they have caused them. This is a contentious position because 'fault' implies, if not intention, at least the power of the person at fault to avoid the harmful action, and it is debatable whether the social structure can be described in this way.

There are people who benefit from past injustice. Nozick argues, for example, for 'rectificatory justice' for the American Indians to redress the wrongs that their ancestors suffered (Nozick 1974). Why should people feel any obligation for the actions of past generations? This is linked with an ancient and strongly felt association of the individual with a family, tribe, or nation; it is the act of one group which compensates another. Once again, it is difficult to see compensation of this type in terms of 'fault'. Some people are poor because of historic injustice – like colonial exploitation or lost wars – but the harm could not have been avoided by the people to whom the responsibility is now attributed.

Finally, there is a view that all of us must pay. This may be because 'we are all guilty' as members of society; an alternative view is that we are paying, not because we are in any sense 'responsible', but because the distribution of resources within a society cannot be justified on proportionate grounds. It returns, again, to Tawney's central point: the fact that society is a certain way does not make it right.

JUSTICE AND DISABILITY

An example of the complex nature of systems for redistribution is the provision of financial support for disability, which Brown calls 'the disability income system' (Brown 1984). Disability is a portmanteau term, covering a wide variety of different conditions and issues. Townsend identifies several main uses of the word (Townsend 1979). A disability may be 'an anatomical, physiological or psychological abnormality or loss' (*ibid.*: 686) – a person missing an arm or an eye, a person with a curved spine, a mentally handicapped child, or a psychiatric patient with schizophrenia. This definition is used to identify 'disability' for the purposes of Industrial Disablement Benefit; a person who has become completely deaf is 100 per cent disabled, the loss of an arm is 70 to 90 per cent, the loss of a big toe is 14 per cent, and the tip of a little finger is 2 per cent.

Disability can also be 'a chronic clinical condition altering or interrupting physiological or psychological process' (*ibid.*: 686). This may include a number of the cases above – like deafness or a curved spine – as well as problems like bronchitis, arthritis, and ulcers. But it excludes a number of other problems, like the loss of a finger, which are not necessarily 'disabling' in the sense of constituting either a medical problem or an interference in the way people live their lives. Mobility Allowance is given to those who are virtually unable to walk, but they must show an organic reason for the handicap; mentally handicapped people who have not learnt to walk do not qualify if there is no attributable physical reason for their handicap.

Although this definition is still primarily based on physical or mental differences, the ways in which the term is defined begin to reflect social issues. Townsend's third definition is disability as a 'functional limitation of ordinary activity' (*ibid.*: 686). Here the emphasis falls not so much on the physical or mental problems in themselves as in the way in which they affect the person's ability to act. Attendance Allowance is available to people who are severely disabled and need frequent or prolonged attention as a result. Functional disability is also a criterion for Industrial Disablement Benefit or compensation in the courts. But the 'attention' people need, or the extent to which their behaviour is changed, depends on their ability to manage with impairment; people respond to incontinence or the loss of limbs in very different ways. However, if disability is defined by the way in which people are able to function in response to a condition, it is the response rather than the condition which is the crucial factor.

Disability can next be represented as a socially defined pattern of behaviour. Whether people are regarded as 'disabled' is as much a matter of social convention as it is of physical capacity. A young person who cannot manage stairs may be treated as 'disabled' when an old person is not. Mentally handicapped people are often treated as 'disabled' even though they may have a demonstrable capacity to work. Social norms determine a person's pattern of behaviour, and it is behaviour, not the physiological or psychological cause, which defines someone as being disabled.

Lastly, Townsend argues that disabled people are a class – a group of people identified by their common social and economic circumstances, sharing the experience of 'being disabled'. This is more a political position than a definition – a case for the provision of welfare for disabled people on a unified basis in place of the fragmentary and uncoordinated series of benefits that are currently available.

The criteria on which disabled people currently receive income support are varied and often inconsistent. There is a principle of *insurance*. People who have contributed to a social-insurance fund, and whose career is interrupted by chronic sickness or disability, receive Invalidity Benefit. This has proved to be an inadequate basis for provision, because many disabled people are unable to contribute.

There are the benefits Brown refers to as *employment-based* (Brown 1984, Ch. 7). Permanent health insurance, occupational pensions, and sick pay play an important role; sick pay alone, Brown suggests, provides 15 per cent of all compensation for injury. The principle here is not so much one of insurance – which implies a pooled risk – as contractual protection. The objections to this are, first, that it favours most those who are better off to begin with and, second, that most disabled people are in no position to protect themselves in this way.

Disabled people may receive benefits according to *financial need*. Claimants of Supplementary Benefit received additions for problems arising out of their disability, including allowances for laundry, heating, and special clothing. This provision, abolished in 1988, suffered from two principal problems: it was means-tested, attracting the usual opprobrium associated with the practice, and it involved intrusive and degrading inquiries. 'It cannot be right', a recent government paper argued, 'to have rules which lead to officials asking claimants how many baths a week they have been advised to take' (Cmnd 9518, 1985: 21). There are now, in their place, premiums for disabled people who receive Income Support. Another way of meeting financial need is represented by Severe Disablement Allowance, which covers those at least 80 per cent disabled who are unable to work and not covered by insurance benefits. The need recognized here is caused by the inability to earn; the 80 per cent criterion is less a recognition of the special needs of severely disabled people than a limitation of claims from others, less severely disabled, who are also unable to work.

Benefits like Attendance Allowance and Mobility Allowance, on the face of it, provide for extraordinary financial needs. But they are not related to income or wealth. The claimants of Attendance Allowance are disabled people, not the people who care for them; the disabled people do not have to have anyone who might look after them. Nor is there any requirement for Mobility Allowance to be used for the provision of transport. It is difficult to be certain exactly what the principle is behind these benefits. They are effectively allowances for certain types of disablement treated according to the extent of incapacity, limited in their scope by the imposition of fairly restrictive criteria. The true justification for the benefits seems to be a recognition of *disability as a category of need in itself* – not simply as a condition creating financial problems.

There is the principle of *rehabilitation*, assisting disabled people to participate fully in social life – in practice, tending to mean rehabilitation for employment. There is a 'quota' of jobs which large firms are supposedly expected to fill with disabled employees; claimants of Invalidity Benefit are allowed the concession of earnings from 'therapeutic' work; disabled workers can receive assistance with taxi fares to work if they are unable to use public transport. This seems, in a different way from insurance, to stress a contribution to society.

There is a *reward for desert*. War disablement pensions were introduced in 1917; the scheme continues to be rather more generous than other benefits.

Lastly, there is a principle of *compensation for disability*. A person who is disabled through someone else's fault, say in road traffic accidents, can sue in the courts for compensation. People injured by criminal activity can receive damages equivalent to those awarded in civil cases. Industrial disablement benefit offers a financial return for even small physical losses. The basis of compensation is not need or desert but 'justice' of a simpler kind – restitution for harm.

There is one principle notably absent from this list – distribution on the basis of rights. The Disability Alliance have argued for a unified benefit for disabled people, available as of right to all, irrespective of income or wealth – in other words, a universal benefit. In practice, benefits for the disabled fall so far short of this ideal as to make it seem utopian. Most disabled people in Britain, and particularly most severely disabled people, are old (Harris 1971). But the benefits are often aimed at younger people – there are age limits on Mobility Allowance, Invalidity Benefit, and Severe Disablement Allowance, and work-related benefits are mainly irrelevant to the problems of elderly disabled people. The expansion of the benefits system to cover the disabled population universally would involve a massively increased commitment to provision for the disabled, a commitment which seems unlikely to be made in the foreseeable future.

The distribution of resources and services to disabled people is not a case for equality. Although there is a presumption of equality in cases which are like each other, the application of different criteria will clearly create advantages for some people over others. Justice for the disabled is not a simple or straightforward issue. A universal benefit would have to balance competing claims on the basis of rights, need, desert, and compensation – not to mention the payment of benefits on other grounds, like charity, personal development, and payments intended to reduce the burden of support borne by the others in society. The provision of welfare is, perhaps inevitably, a compromise between conflicting principles.

XII

Structural policy

Summary: *Structural policy is the attempt to deliberately change a society. It may be done by aiming for an ideal model; by pragmatic, incremental change; or by reference to principles as guides for action.*

'Justice' seems, to its critics, to offer the potential for almost unlimited state intervention in social life. Hayek suggests that 'Once government has embarked upon planning for the sake of justice, it cannot refuse responsibility for anybody's fate or position' (Hayek 1944: 80). This is almost right. The idea of social justice, like the argument for equality, rests on the belief that moral arguments must be applied to the organization of society. If, as Hayek suggests, 'no free action of . . . individuals could produce results satisfying any principle of distributive justice' (Hayek 1976: 69), then some intervention is necessary. Because governments cannot avoid moral responsibility for the distribution of resources in society, they must form some plan of how those resources are to be distributed. In other words, they must have a policy for society.

Ferge distinguishes 'social' from 'societal', or 'structural', policy. Social policy is policy for social welfare, and concentrates mainly on the social services. Structural policy 'implies the project of deliberately changing the profile of a society, of altering basic human, social relations' (Ferge 1979: 55). Townsend argues, I think rightly, that social policy is as much concerned with structural policy as with the study of social welfare. He suggests that social policy

> can be defined as *the underlying as well as the professed rationale by which social institutions and groups are used or brought into being to ensure social preservation or development*. Social policy is, in other words, the institutionalised control of agencies and organisations to maintain or change social structure and values.
>
> (Townsend 1976: 6)

This is framed in the same terms as Ferge's idea, but it differs in two respects. First, whereas Ferge is concerned only with social change (and asserts that western societies have no structural policy), Townsend extends the definition to include policies which maintain social order. This seems irresistible, because order and change are two sides of the same coin. Second, Ferge suggests that policy has to be deliberate; Townsend argues that it can be implicit, 'unspoken and even unrecognised' (*ibid.*: 6). I think this goes too far; although policies may be interpreted as 'implicit', it is in the nature of policy that it is in some sense intentional. This does not mean that government must explicitly intervene in every aspect of social life, but only that the implications for justice of both action and non-action must at least have been considered.

Social welfare may be seen as structural in itself; the very idea of a 'welfare state' suggests that developments in the social services have brought about some change in society. It may be structural in an instrumental sense, because of its implications for other aspects of society. The monitoring of mothers by health visitors can be seen as a reinforcement of certain values about the family, the administration of benefits for unemployed people as a method of stressing the work ethic. Social welfare may be a cause of change, like programmes of clearance and urban renewal. It can be a means of facilitating change, for example the introduction of free primary education, which helped to make a literate workforce. And it may, perhaps, be a consequence of it: Titmuss argues that changes in wartime created a collectivist spirit which made the welfare state possible (Titmuss 1955b). It may be all of these; it can be argued that the introduction of universal free secondary education in 1944 was a consequence of changes in the war, contributed to the growth of a professional class, and it can be argued, through its emphasis on 'merit', led to other changes in order to promote 'equality of opportunity'.

The interpretation of policy is difficult and contentious. Policy may be explicit or implicit; it may be in the interests of various individuals, groups, communities, or classes; its effects may be inconsistent with its objectives. Social welfare policy is structural either when it is explicitly directed at structural change, or when it actually achieves such an effect. (It may be possible to argue that a policy was implicitly structural but had not worked; this seems to me impossible to prove.) Many social welfare policies have been explicitly devoted to either the maintenance or the change of the social structure. Council housing, in 1919, was intended (at least in part) to avert a revolution. The introduction of comprehensive education was intended, by the Labour government, to reform the class system. The expansion of the personal social services in the early 1970s was encouraged on the basis that it would break the 'cycle of deprivation'. The US War on Poverty aimed to co-opt blacks into the political process. The introduction of Supplementary Benefit in 1966 was intended to remove the stigma of claiming and establish income maintenance as a right of citizenship.

The effectiveness of these policies is difficult to judge. There was no revolution after the First World War, but it is impossible to say whether this had anything to do with council housing – like the man in the joke who paints white lines on roads to keep the elephants away. The War on Poverty was followed by the inclusion of more blacks in politics, but it is impossible to say that this would not have happened without the programme. The success or failure of a policy depends crucially on the causal analysis applied. It is difficult to assess the ability of the social services to deal with the 'cycle of deprivation' when there is now fairly good evidence that the cycle does not exist in any generally applicable sense (Brown and Madge 1982). And the problems of stigma associated with benefits are, I have argued elsewhere, much deeper and more complex than the simplistic attempt to create 'rights' suggests (Spicker 1984).

The explicit reasons for policy have to be evaluated, then, in the light of causal explanations for change. Implicit reasons are generally also attributed to policy-makers on causal criteria – for example, by explanations like those of Bachrach and Baratz, based on their view of the distribution of power in society. Equally, structural changes which occur without conscious intention, implicitly or otherwise, could only be analysed in structural terms. It seems to follow that it is the explanation of the process, rather than the motivation, which is doing the work in defining a policy as 'structural'. This is not to say that the explicit reasons for a policy are unimportant – they are a major part of the criteria by which policies can be judged – but they are not the most important issues in this context.

THE NATURE OF SOCIAL CHANGE

The idea of 'society' describes a complex network of relationships. The 'structure' of society is an analytical construct, an interpretation of social relationships as a pattern, and the test of social change is whether the pattern is altered. This requires a view of the process in historical terms. One way of doing this is *historicism* – the term was coined by Karl Popper (1945). The core of historicism is the belief that historical events are causally related and patterned. They are, therefore, predictable. Historicism interprets social change in terms of a sequence of forms of social structure. The welfare state, for example, is sometimes seen as an intermediate stage between capitalism and socialism. The value of historicism is that it focuses attention on major, long-term movements. Its main weaknesses are that it may lead to some fairly superficial generalizations, that it oversimplifies the nature of social change, and, for what it is worth, that it is very debatable whether any historicist predictions are actually right.

Societies are often referred to in terms of 'ideal types', models which reality may or may not conform to. As long as a society can be compared to the model in its basic essentials, it can reasonably be described in those terms. Even though there may be changes in the pattern of social relationships, they may fail to alter fundamental structures; so, for example, the United Kingdom is still regarded by many as 'capitalist' despite the alterations of the last 150 years. Crosland outlines the main features of 'capitalism' as *laissez faire*, the domination of market forces; the ownership of industry by private individuals; the control of industry by a class of owner-managers; the concentration of economic power in the hands of one class; an ideology of individualism, competition, and the value of private property; and an intense conflict between classes. He argues that all of these have ceased, to a large extent, to be true (Crosland 1956, Ch. 3). Certainly, there are elements of this model in present-day society, but there are elements of many other models, too; the effect of the 'ideal type' is to pass over other aspects of social relationships which might not fit the particular perspective. It is a blinkered way of looking at the world.

The idea of 'family resemblance' is, I suggested in Chapter 6, a less misleading way of describing things. The effect of taking this approach is that it is no longer necessary to ask whether society conforms 'in essence' to a particular model. If society now can be described as 'capitalist', it is not because it conforms in greater or lesser degree to an ideal model; it is because of its immediate resemblance to its capitalist antecedents, and to other societies described in similar terms. (It could equally be argued that since there is little resemblance between societies which are only distant relatives in the family, or at the beginning and end of a long period of time, the label doesn't mean a lot; this is a matter of perspective.)

If this approach is accepted, there is no need to refer to the 'fundamental' elements of a society. Changes are constantly taking place, and though alterations in patterns may be imperceptible at any one point in time, a comparison of social structures over a longer period may well show important differences. This means that any change can be seen as contributing to the maintenance or change of a social structure, and so that social welfare policy can be seen as a form of structural policy in itself. At first sight, this seems almost trivial, but it has important substantive implications. Social welfare does have a potential for change; but a new pattern might develop without anyone planning it and without any decision-maker taking an overview. The test of social welfare policy is not, then, whether it alters social relations; it is how it alters them.

STRATEGIES FOR CHANGE

Even if social policies cause changes, it it not easy to harness them to bring about directed changes. People are not always consistent in what they want; for example, bloc-regarding equality and person-regarding equality may yield contradictory results. People may not agree about what the change should be: opposition or conflict may lead to compromise, or a solution which satisfies no-one – like the programmes of Urban Renewal in the United States, which offered only partial concessions to black groups. Besides, the capacity of planners to predict outcomes is limited because our understanding of social processes is incomplete. It is possible to predict the number of old people in the future with reasonable accuracy, given certain reservations, and this has major implications for social services and society as a whole. But the ways in which services are provided for old people could also be affected by changes in aspirations, the demands made by other dependent groups, the politics of old age (like a Grey Panther movement, perhaps), the status of women, and other changes in policies for old people – like health, retirement, financial support, or euthanasia.

Some critics see this uncertainty as an objection to any sort of planned change, and attempts to prove that welfare provisions have had unexpectedly negative consequences abound. They are not always well chosen. Herbert Spencer, for example, wrote:

> When, under the New Poor Law, provision was made for the accommodation of vagrants in the Union-houses, it was hardly expected that a body of tramps would be thereby called into existence, who would spend their time in walking from Union to Union throughout the kingdom. . . . Thus on all sides are well meant measures producing unforeseen mischiefs.
>
> (Spencer, quoted in Bramsted and Melhuish 1978: 638)

This, to borrow a phrase, is like blaming wig-makers for baldness. Another misconceived illustration is the accusation that the Rent Acts in the United Kingdom have caused the decline of the private rented sector (see e.g. Seldon 1977, Ch. 6). This overlooks a few details, like increased finance for owner-occupation, competition from public-sector housing, the disappearing demand for renting which resulted, the availability of alternative investments, diminishing returns on capital, and the increasing costs of maintaining an ageing stock of houses, which can largely account for the effect without reference to rent control. There are better cases, though none is uncontentious – they all deal in speculations about what might have happened if history had been different. Prohibition in the United States not only failed to have the desired effect but seems to have generated undesired and unexpected consequences by financing organized crime. The effect of the 1969 Children and Young Persons Act, which attempted to remove the stigma of criminality from young offenders, may well have been to extend the stigma to other children in care. And the expansion of higher education in the United Kingdom in the 1960s can be argued to have worsened the relative position of the working-class children it was supposed to help. If one was to take the view that society was a valuable and delicate mechanism, like a precision watch, these arguments might be persuasive; but the risk of doing something wrong is not necessarily a good reason for not trying to do it right.

There are three main approaches to 'structural' policy. One view is that structural policy is intended to create a wholly new social structure. This is, I think, implicit in Ferge's argument that western societies have no structural policy. It is not that they do not have policies which attempt to change or maintain social relationships, but rather that the policies are not thought of as part of a progression towards an ideal. According to this view, structural policy means that alterations are made by trying to conform to certain models. Townsend writes that social policy 'is best conceived as a kind of blueprint for the management of society towards social ends' (Townsend 1976: 6). This is sometimes referred to as 'social engineering'; it implies that there is an ideal pattern of a new society which is the aim of social reform. Examples of this kind of reform have included the aims of the French Revolution and the origins of the Soviet Union. Lesser attempts – hardly less daring in their way – are Le Corbusier's 'Ville Radieuse' or Howard's Garden Cities movement, ideas which have profoundly affected approaches to urban planning (see Hall 1975, Ch. 3).

There are several problems with this approach. Hall argues about the early planners that

> Their vision seems to have been that of the planner as omniscient ruler, who would create new settlement forms, and perhaps also destroy the old, without interference or question. There was one true vision of the future world as it ought to be, and each of them saw himself as its prophet. . . . there is an evident risk of a stifling orthodoxy.
>
> (Hall 1975: 79)

Blueprints often ignore the realities of the social conditions on which the ideals are imposed. The problems of high-rise buildings reflected insufficient consideration of the poverty of the tenants, the ability of designers to achieve the aims at the intended cost, or the aspirations of many people for a differing kind of housing. The NHS had an inheritance of outdated buildings, maldistribution of resources, a model of medicine as a scientific, curative activity, and an increasing number of old people in bad health. Edmund Burke warns, 'The science of constructing a commonwealth, or renovating it, or reforming it, is, like every other experimental science, not to be taught *à priori*' (Burke 1790: 72).

This is the foundation of the conservative case against structural policy. The conservative view, Barry writes, is that 'all attempts to transform societies in accordance with principles . . . are pernicious' (Barry 1965: 54). The most powerful objection comes from those who believe that planning is unjustified on moral grounds. There is an individualist element in much conservative writing, which leads to resistance to attempts to impose morals and norms on other people by means of the state. Hayek argues that no-one has the right to interfere with individual freedom when the basis of social planning is necessarily uncertain (Hayek 1976: 2). Whether this point of view is accepted depends on the relative value of liberty and the other principles which inform social policy.

The second view of structural policy is based on what Steenbergen calls a 'push' rather than a 'pull' model (Steenbergen 1983). 'Pull' models are those in which change is directed to an end. 'Push' models see change as a process firmly rooted in past circumstances. The structure of families, the number of dependants, the health of the population, the factories, farms, roads, schools, and hospitals already in existence, limit the scope of possible change and determine to a large extent the pattern of the future. The approach which is prompted by this view is a pragmatic one. Burke recommends gradual, incremental change, ensuring each step is firm before proceeding to the next. Reforms must be partial, limited, and carefully examined before the next step is taken (Burke 1790: 209). The advantages of this approach is that it recognizes the limitations imposed by present realities, that it builds on the lessons of the past, that it avoids the disastrous effects of major social experiments which go wrong. The disadvantages are that it is very slow, and that piecemeal reforms may lead over time to a complex, incomprehensible hotchpotch of services. The obvious illustration of this is the UK social-security system (see Dilnot, Kay, and Morris 1984).

The third view of structural policy sees it as an attempt to change relations in accordance with principles rather than ideals. The

distinction between these two is often blurred. A person who pursues
an ideal proceeds by identifying the end; an emphasis on principles
means that it is necessary to judge the action in itself. Society is
altered, not by reconstruction but by regulating and changing
relationships on moral grounds. This is typified by Crosland's
approach to equality:

> We can . . . describe the direction of advance, and even discern the
> landscape ahead; but the ultimate objective lies wrapped in
> uncertainty. This must be the case unless one subscribes to the
> vulgar fallacy that some ideal society can be said to exist, of which
> blueprints can be drawn. . . . socialism is not an exact descriptive
> term, connoting a particular social structure, past, present or even
> immanent in some sage's mind, which can be empirically observed
> or even analysed. It simply describes a set of values, or aspirations,
> which socialists wish to see embodied in the organisation of society.
>   (Crosland 1956: 216)

The search for greater equality of opportunity, for redistribution of
resources, or a right to work are principles of this type. They have
informed policies, respectively, or comprehensive education, progressive taxation, and job creation. These examples come from one
side of the political spectrum, but it is important to recognize that the
Conservative government under Mrs Thatcher is just as committed
to principled reform; the stress on property, family values, and
independence from state intervention can be seen in the encouragement of owner-occupation, policies for community care, and the
encouragement of private non-statutory provision.

The obvious objection to an approach based on principles is that it
is too vague to be useful. There may be conflicts between principles
which it is almost impossible to resolve satisfactorily: should one
allocate resources according to rights, to work, or to need? Even if
there is broad agreement about principles, there is not necessarily a
consensus about which policy is best. And the result of following
disparate principles in all directions may be, not an advance, but a
quagmire in which the effects of one policy cancel out the effects of
another. The conflict between universality and progressive redistribution, if one accepts Le Grand's argument, is a possible example.

The distinction between reform through ideals and principles seems to me useful mainly as a means of distinguishing the intentions of those who want to bring about changes in society. In practice, however, the two are difficult to separate. It may be that, by striving for principles – like civil liberties, decent housing, or free education – that one is able to establish conditions which others would describe as ideal. It is quite possible to strive for an ideal while seeking to ensure that each step is consistent with basic values. And it is possible to aim for an ideal and to discover, in the end, that one has only established a principle instead. This fate befell the British NHS, which was supposed to end disease and abolish inequalities in health and achieved in their place universal coverage as a right of citizenship – a point which is far from negligible but which falls well short of the ideal.

Each of these strategies has strong merits and demerits; each, in different contexts, has some value. Personally, I lean towards principled change – as the tenor and content of the book might suggest. The study of social policy is in large part based on attempts to make people's lives better – to increase their welfare. Reformers are sometimes accused of 'shifting the deckchairs around on the Titanic'. Even if we are on the Titanic, which I doubt, there is nothing wrong, and much right, in making people comfortable. It may be for the short term, but in the long run, as Keynes remarked, we are all dead. Social welfare may be a consequence of change, but it can also be a means of change in itself. In doing so, it has the potential directly to change the structure of a society – even if the results are not immediately obvious.

PART 3

Conclusion

XIII

Ideologies of welfare

Summary: *Principles are not formed randomly; they occur in ideologies, interrelated sets of ideas, like 'conservatism' and 'socialism'. But these doctrines are more complex than they are often presented, and there are contradictions in the positions people hold. An understanding of principles is essential to understand the way people actually think.*

The concepts discussed in this book are interrelated; it is often difficult to separate moral principles from issues like rights and freedom, or justice and the state from democracy and citizenship. In part, this happens because practical problems raise not one but many issues. But much of it is intrinsic to the ideas themselves; there are clear, direct connections between them. The view that people take of redistribution is going to be affected by their views of freedom, morality, altruism, rights, citizenship, the state, power, equality, and justice; equally, all of these concepts are affected by at least some of the others. This means that ideas tend to be formed into systems of thought rather than randomly; the principles inform and reinforce each other.

Mishra outlines three common sets of views, which he refers to as 'residual', 'institutional', and 'socialist' (Mishra 1981). Mishra's presentation shows these models as differing not so much in fundamentals as in degree (Table 13.1). This reflects a common view of the historical sequence through which the UK 'welfare state' was formed. It seems possible to slide from one model into the next – consistent with the view that the 'welfare state' is a stage on the road to socialism. But a description of a process of changing views and policy cannot easily be extended to a discussion of principles. It is difficult to see how one could slide from one principle to another – from the individual model of freedom to a social model, or from a view of justice as based in desert to one based in need.

Table 13.1 *Three models of welfare*

	Residual	Institutional	Socialist
Attitudes to:			
State intervention	Minimal	Optimal	Total
Need as basis of provision	Marginal	Secondary	Primary
Range of services	Limited	Extensive	Comprehensive
Population covered	Minority	Majority	All
Level of benefits	Low	Medium	High
% of national income spent on welfare	Low	Medium	High
Means testing	Primary	Secondary	Marginal
Clients	Paupers	Citizens	Members of collective
Status of clients	Low	Medium	High
Orientation	Coercive	Utilitarian	Solidaristic
Role of non-state services	Primary	Secondary	Marginal

Source: Mishra 1981: 101–34.

On closer examination, the impression that is created of a progression is largely based on a misinterpretation of the meaning of 'institutional welfare'. Institutional welfare does not treat needs as 'secondary' and does not cover only the 'majority' of the population. In Titmuss's descriptions of the institutional model, everyone is seen as liable to be in need at some point, and so everyone benefits, as a citizen, through the provision of social services which guarantee essential care (Titmuss 1974). This principle is fundamental to the idea of the 'welfare state'. Clearly, if institutional welfare was interpreted in this way, it would overlap with Mishra's 'socialist' model. However, there is an important distinction to be made between the two. The socialist model, in common with institutional views of welfare, emphasizes elements of solidarity and implies that benefits will be paid at an optimal level. But the orientation of a 'socialist' system is liable to be egalitarian as well as solidaristic, and whereas in the welfare state resources are redistributed to protect citizens and offer social security (in its widest sense) as a right, in a socialist model the distribution of resources is organized according to

Table 13.2 *Patterns of welfare in three ideal types of society*

Ideal type of society	Hierarchical	Individualist	Collectivist
Unit of social organization	Family	Individual	Community
Status of the individual	Duty-bound	Independent	Citizen
Political organization	Aristocracy	Representative democracy	Participative democracy
Moral basis of welfare	Charity	Residual	Institutional
Form of welfare	Voluntary/ occupational	Selective	Universal
Form of exchange	Ritualized	Balanced	Generalized
Form of stigma	Caste	Individual	Social
Interpretation of freedom	Duty	Individual	Social
Basis of justice	Status	Desert	Need
Basis of rights	Ascribed	Acquired	Universal

an egalitarian concept of social justice. Institutional welfare is not, then, simply a stage which is intermediate between residual and socialist models; it might more accurately be described as an alternative to either.

A modified version of Mishra's approach is suggested by David Miller's method, in *Social Justice* (Miller 1976). Miller identifies the different ideas of justice with different models of society. The *hierarchical* or feudal society is characterized by rigid social divisions, and the concept of justice implies distribution according to status. The *market* society is individualistic and competitive; justice is based in desert, measured by the rewards people receive in competition with others. In the *collectivist* society, rights and responsibilities are shared equally by everyone as members of a community. (Miller refers to this as a 'primitive' society, because it is only in primitive societies that a high degree of collectivism and mutual support has existed; it is more usual to see this referred to as 'socialist'.) A just distribution is made according to need.

These are ideal types of society – models against which reality can be compared (Table 13.2); they should not be confused with reality itself, which shows features of each type, and perhaps of others too. The problems associated with this method were commented on in

Chapter 6. Their value is that they provide a way of presenting different approaches to welfare, in which the various ideas form a clear and distinct pattern.

The different societies are associated not just with different ideas but with different systems of thought. The hierarchical society depends crucially on concepts of duty – duty to the family, to people above oneself in the hierarchy – welfare is based on the duties of the donor, not the rights of the recipient. The individualist society emphasizes independence and competition; welfare is for those who fail in the competitive market. The collectivist society stresses solidarity and mutual support.

This helps to emphasize that advocates of different principles may have, not simply different values, but different models of society in mind. In real life, society does not conform to the ideal types, and the effect can be that policies predicated on the assumptions of one ideal have unexpected consequences when they are put into practice. One example of this is the imposition of penalties for not working. This may be justifiable in a competitive society in which people are able to succeed by virtue of increased effort; it is hardly defensible at a time when there is little work available for people who are unemployed. Another example, from a different ideological perspective, is the provision for needs on the institutional basis associated with collectivist ideals. In an equal society, provision on the grounds of need would preserve equality of outcome. But in a society which is not equal, people who are sick, disabled, having children, or going on to higher education, may well be better off than others, and perhaps even better off than the people who pay.

The impact of this kind of approach can be seen clearly in debates on social security, where there has been a continuing dispute between advocates of universal and selective benefits. Universality is linked with institutional welfare because the idea that everyone is in need at some time is linked with the idea that everyone should benefit. Selectivity is linked with residual welfare because the idea of a 'safety net' implies a concentration on those in need. The models are in turn commonly linked to attitudes towards the private market. Some writers, like Hayek and Friedman, are against state intervention in principle, and believe that welfare should be confined to a safety net so that intervention is reduced to a minimum. This position links selectivity, residualism, and the private sector. Others, like Crosland and Titmuss, believe that services should be publicly provided on an institutional basis and see the state as the best way to do this.

However, this is not the only way that the ideas could be lined up. Universality and selectivity are *methods* of distribution, not models, and either could be consistent with residual or institutional welfare. One could favour institutional welfare and selectivity – like Marx's 'to each according to his needs' – or residual welfare and universality, because one believes universality (like the provision of general housing subsidies, for example) is a better way to provide a safety net against poverty. Equally, a person may believe in institutional welfare and hold that the private market is still a better way than the state to distribute certain resources, like food, if only people are given the money. Cash support in any form implicitly favours the private sector, in the sense that people are given money to spend rather than goods or services (like health and education). On the other hand, a person who believes that welfare should only be given to those in need may favour giving people the goods rather than money. One may reasonably argue for public heating schemes rather than heating allowances on social security.

In general, because of the associations of the ideas, the British Labour Party has tended to favour universal views and a resistance to means-testing; the Conservatives have moved towards a residual model with means tests that 'target' resources on those who are poorest. Since 1970, Conservative governments have been responsible for Family Income Supplement/Family Credit, Housing Benefit, and two major reforms of Supplementary Benefit/Income Support; Labour for non-contributory benefits for disabled people, and Child Benefit. Child Benefit is an important benefit, particularly for women. But three-quarters of Child Benefit goes to people above the Income Support level, and because Child Benefit is deducted directly from the means-tested benefits, it is worthless to those who do receive Income Support. The benefit is represented nevertheless as a major contribution towards the condition of the poor. This seems to be based on the validity of universality as part of an institutional model rather than on the actual effect it has. By contrast, means-testing, at it simplest level, is a way of redistributing money directly to the poor, and the most effective way of improving the condition of the poorest people in the United Kingdom tomorrow would be to increase the level of Income Support, which is the most important means-tested benefit. But means-testing in general, and dependence on Income Support in particular, is staunchly opposed by the left wing. The political debate seems to have been based on the models which different methods are supposed to represent rather than the actual effects that measures will have. It appears from this example that an understanding of systems of thought is crucial for an understanding of the policy debate; it is not possible to make sense of it in terms of the principles alone.

IDEOLOGY AND WELFARE

These systems of thought are referred to as *ideologies*, sets of interrelated concepts. Ideologies, Eccleshall writes, 'share two principal characteristics: an image of society and a political programme. . . . An ideology . . . provides a coherent perspective through which to understand and act upon the social world' (Eccleshall *et al.* 1984: 8). The seminal text written in these terms is by Victor George and Paul Wilding (1977). They distinguish four main ideological positions. *Marxists* see society in terms of a conflict between economic classes, and their analysis of welfare concentrates principally on its relationship to the exercise of power. *Fabians*, characterized by Titmuss, Tawney, and Crosland, are socialists who believe in the gradual reform of society, and see welfare as a principal means of achieving greater social equality. The '*reluctant collectivists*' (Keynes, Galbraith, and Beveridge) accept the 'mixed economy'; the welfare state is a necessary corrective to the failures of a competitive market to provide security and to meet basic needs. Fourth, there are the '*anti-collectivists*', like Hayek and Friedman, who value individual freedom and private enterprise, and see the growing welfare state as a threat to the autonomy and independence of the citizen.

Much of the appeal of George and Wilding's analysis is that it helps to identify ideologies with the conventional distinctions between 'left', 'centre', and 'right'. 'Left' and 'right' are fairly vague terms, associated as much with people's political affiliations as with the beliefs they hold (the labels are said to come originally from where people sat in the French national assembly). A person who is 'left' wing stands for socialism, against the free market, for the working class, and greater equality of result. A person who is 'right' wing is an individualist, in favour of the free market, a defender of the way things are and so of the interests of those who currently gain most from society. The political 'centre' stands between them, favouring a mixed economy, individual rights, and collective action.

George and Wilding suggest that 'what ultimately divides our four groups of thinkers in their social values is their differing views about freedom and equality' (George and Wilding 1977: 128). But the ideas of freedom and equality, as they describe them, are in turn dependent on views of society, the state, and the economy. The view of freedom expressed by the 'anti-collectivists' is not only a model of individual freedom, but one which is linked to the concept of the free-market economy, and a primary justification for inequality is that in a free economy people will be unequal. By contrast, Marxists, at the other end of the spectrum, see freedom 'in terms of the removal of obstacles to human emancipation and self-realisation' (*ibid.*: 97), and they view the economic organization of capitalist society as being inimical to these values.

George and Wilding's approach has been enormously influential; a similar pattern of argument can be seen in a number of texts (e.g. Room 1979; Taylor-Gooby and Dale 1981; Mishra 1981; Open University 1985). The advantage of this kind of analysis is that it helps to explain the way that people think about welfare issues. It draws out the interrelationships between ideas; it helps to explain why people choose some ideas rather than others; and it presents theoretical material in a fairly accessible form. But it can also conceal as much as it reveals. The approach is, in important respects, alarmingly misleading. George and Wilding's classification of ideologies is seen very much from the perspective of the left, and they have overestimated the importance of extremes, seriously oversimplified the range of possible views, and caricatured the political centre, who are labelled with the disparaging title of 'reluctant collectivists' to suggest that they haven't really made their mind up. It would take another book to set this properly to rights, but it is possible here at least to mark out some of the territory that needs to be covered in the context of welfare provision in the United Kingdom.

The divisions within and between different ideological positions are blurred by the necessity of co-operating with others in order to achieve political ends. The British political parties are not unified groups seeking to achieve common aims, but coalitions of people with different interests, attitudes, and opinions. The Labour Party, Crosland argues, shows the influence of at least twelve ideological positions (Crosland 1956, Ch. 4):

(1) *The philosophy of natural law.* Natural law, in the English tradition, emphasized personal freedom and the right of labour to property.
(2) *Owenism.* Owenism aimed for a peaceful, enlightened reform of the industrial system on the principle of co-operation in a classless society.
(3) *Marxism.*
(4) *Syndicalism*, or workers' control. This is strongly associated with the trend to participative democracy.
(5) *Guild socialism.* This differed from syndicalism in its mistrust of state authority, and emphasis on libertarianism.
(6) *Christian socialism.* Christian socialism deplored the ethic of the competitive society and emphasized human rights and moral duties to the rest of humankind.
(7) *The labour theory of value.* The view that labour is the source of all value, and so that employment is exploitative, is now commonly associated with Marxism; but it developed separately from Marxism, and in fact Marx himself made important criticisms of the popular doctrine (Marx 1875).
(8) *The theory of rent as unearned increment.* This is Crosland's term for the reaction against unearned income from land ownership, a view which led to calls for public ownership of land.
(9) *Fabianism.* Fabianism is an intellectual movement stressing gradual reform, expansion of collective action through the role of the state, and egalitarianism as something which is both morally superior and increases social welfare overall.
(10) *William Morris and anti-commercialism.* Morris aimed for a utopian 'back to nature' society – a reaction against the degrading conditions of those involved in industrial production.

(11) *The ILP*. This was, Crosland suggests, based on ideas of the 'brotherhood of man, fellowship, service and altruism' (*ibid.*: 85).

(12) *The welfare state and paternalism*. This tradition accepted the responsibility of the state for the provision of welfare. The doctrine of planning, which Crosland sees as a separate trend in socialist thought, seems to stem from the same belief in the role of the state as the executive arm of social responsibility.

To Crosland's catalogue, I would add at least three more traditions:

(13) *Levelling*. The repudiation of privilege.

(14) *Keynesian economics*. Keynes wrote that 'The outstanding faults of the economic society in which we live are its failure to provide for full employment and its arbitrary and inequitable distribution of income' (Keynes 1936: 372). He made the case that 'the duty of ordering the current volume of investment cannot safely be left in private hands' (*ibid.*: 320) and argued that 'I expect to see the State, which is in a position to calculate the marginal efficiency of capital-goods on long views and on the basis of general social advantage, taking an even greater responsibility for directly organising investment (*ibid.*: 164). (This is what the writers George and Wilding call a 'reluctant collectivist'.)

(15) *Crosland*. Crosland became a major influence on the Labour Party himself, and his arguments for a strategy of equality through economic growth and educational reform formed a significant element in the interpretation of Labour's role subsequently.

The Conservative tradition is also varied and complex. It includes:

(1) *High Tories*. Tories accept the established order as right and are reluctant to consent to any form of change. An emphasis on traditionalism, religion, and duty are all associated with this view. (For a more detailed examination, see Beer 1982.)

(2) *Old Whigs*. A survival from the days of the landed gentry, there is a tradition of paternal supervision of those less well equipped to manage their affairs. The Old Whig tradition is

associated with the idea of a 'natural aristocracy' which
survived to some extent in Disraeli's thought (see *ibid.*).
(3) *New Whigs*. The philosophy of the 'New Whigs' is best
represented by Edmund Burke. Burke argued that a respect
for tradition was essential – he refers to 'the wisdom of nations
and of ages' – but equally he believed that 'a state without the
means of some change is without the means of its conservation
(Burke 1790: 23). The principle of gradual, pragmatic change
which he favoured (and which was mentioned in the previous
chapter) is seen by some as fundamental to conservatism, and
Burke has been called 'the father of the Conservative Party'.
(4) *Authoritarianism*. An emphasis on social order, militarism, and
firm leadership.
(5) *Economic liberalism*. This is the belief in the free market, and the
minimum of state interference in economic affairs.
(6) *'Social Darwinism'*. This owes little or nothing to Darwin himself.
The idea that society must, like nature, proceed on a principle of
'survival of the fittest' was advocated by Herbert Spencer:

> The poverty of the incapable, the distresses that came upon
> the imprudent, the starvation of the idle, and those
> shoulderings aside of the weak by the strong, which leaves so
> many 'in shallows and in miseries', are the decrees of a large,
> far-seeing benevolence.
>
> (Spencer, quoted in Clinard 1968: 145)

(7) *Political liberalism*. An emphasis on the rights of the individual.
Both major Mental Health Acts since the war, in 1959 and
1983, were passed by Conservative governments. (There is a
clear contradiction here with the authoritarian tendency.)
(8) *Disraeli 'One-nation' conservatism*. All classes, Disraeli argued,
must be given a stake in the country if there is to be unity. This
idea is sometimes represented as the idea of a 'property-
owning democracy' – an idea which has been instrumental in
encouraging the growth of owner-occupation and the extension of share ownership.
(9) *The organic view of society*. 'The Conservative sense of the
historical', Clarke writes, 'leads it to regard society more like a
living organism than a machine' (Clarke 1975: 166). The

metaphor of the organic society is commonly drawn upon in Conservative writing and is used to justify the defence of tradition, national interest, and the emphasis on social unity in 'one nation'.

(10) *Political scepticism.* The belief that society cannot be transformed on the basis of principles is a strong element in Conservative thought from Burke to Oakeshott. The argument is that society is too complex to be meddled with on the basis of a necessarily imperfect understanding.

(11) *Moderation.* The virtues of balance, diversity, compromise, and resistance to extremes are emphasized, for example by Halifax (1684), as desirable in themselves. There is, again, a potential contradiction here with the strongly principled economic and political liberalism found elsewhere in the Conservative tradition. Milton Friedman has commented:

> The thing that people do not recognise is that Margaret Thatcher is not in terms of belief a Tory. She is a nineteenth century Liberal. But her party consists largely of Tories. They don't really believe in free markets. . . . They never have as a party.
>
> (cited Plant 1984)

There is some overlap between Labour and Conservative parties; it can be argued that Crosland's identification of the tradition of the 'welfare state', for example, applies as much to Conservative as to Labour thinking. The other main parties contain elements in common with both Labour and Conservative, and others besides. The Liberal Party, if I understand it correctly, is at times politically (but not economically) liberal, Owenist, moderate, 'green', internationalist, and committed to ideas of 'community politics' and participative democracy. All the main British parties include a strong element of Whiggish pragmatism. This approach emphasizes politics as 'the art of the possible'; it stresses gradual, incremental change, experimentation to find out what works and what does not, and the balance of conflicting interests.

This description of different sets of ideas is limited. It excludes ideologies which have developed outside the main political forum, like feminism or anarchism; many of the intellectual doctrines – like functionalism, utilitarianism, pluralism, or corporatism – referred to in passing in the course of this book; and others besides. But it should be sufficient to show that the construction of welfare ideologies is more complex than the usual descriptions imply. In particular, it should be clear that a number of the views which are commonly associated with one side or another of the political spectrum are more widely held than at first appears.

It is still possible to define political affiliation to some degree by the extent to which people's views conform to a recognizable ideological model. Within the left wing, the dominant models are arguably institutional and collectivist, though there are important differences in opinions about the role of the state and the functions performed by social services. Within the right wing, the main models are residual, individualist, and hierarchical; there are profound differences between traditional conservatism and the radical individualism of the 'new right'. These terms provide a useful shorthand, and a means of understanding people's approaches to welfare. However, the complexity and range of political opinion often make it difficult clearly to identify a person's views on particular issues with an ideological position, and reference to ideologies often has to be treated with caution. In the first place, 'ideology' more often refers to a general approach than to specific details. It would be difficult, from the knowledge that people are 'liberals' or 'Marxists', to work out just what they think about rights or morals; within both approaches there is a wide range of views which overlap as much as they diverge. Second, it can sometimes be difficult to place commentators who are of an individual turn of mind; not all the people who write about social policy buy their ideas off the peg. Although it may be useful at times to refer to certain people as 'left' or 'right', there are more than two dimensions to most of the issues, and there is a danger of misinterpretation. For example, a common objection to the 'free market' system in health care is that poor people would suffer when they could not afford health care. Seldon argues that this confuses equity and efficiency, two quite separate issues (Seldon 1977). Health, he believes, does not have to be publicly provided any more than other necessities, like food or clothing; we can redistribute money to poor people if we want to, and let them spend it as they choose. His position is often met with incomprehension by people who suppose that anyone who advocates a free market has to be against redistribution. I think he is wrong (the arguments are examined in Le Grand and Robinson 1976, Ch. 2), but that is not to say he does not make sense.

Third, there are contradictions in the values people hold. For example, a person may believe in redistribution according to need but will condemn means-testing for being socially divisive. A social worker may argue for 'respect for persons' while demanding that they change, and for self-determination while continuing to intervene if clients seem likely to decide the wrong thing. Some people oppose the sale of council housing on the grounds that the remainder will become 'residual', with large numbers of poor tenants; at the same time, they advocate allocation on the grounds of need, which would increase the proportion of people in council housing who are poor. If we want to understand the positions that people take, it is as important to grasp the basic concepts they are using as the ideologies they are referring to.

An emphasis on principles offers, then, not necessarily a definitive viewpoint, but another way of looking at issues which are basic to the understanding of social policy. This is not to detract from the importance of ideologies. Ideologies, Mannheim argues, are inescapable. None of our values is formed in splendid isolation; in reality, we refer whether we know it or not to certain sets of thought current in society (Mannheim 1936). But ideologies are many and varied; they may be self-contradictory; and the belief that it is necessary to think in terms of a limited range of systems – like Marxism or free-market liberalism – is a grave distortion of the position. The ideologies themselves can best be understood by an analysis of their component elements – the principles of which they are made.

References

Ackerman, B. (1980) *Social Justice in the Liberal State*, New Haven, Conn.: Yale University Press.

Alchian, A. A. and Allen, W. R. (1973) 'The pure economics of giving', in Institute of Economic Affairs, *The Economics of Charity*, London: IEA.

Amdur, R. (1979) 'Compensatory justice: the questions of costs', *Political Theory* 7(2): 229–44.

Arnstein, S. R. (1971) 'A ladder of citizen participation', *Journal of the Royal Town Planning Institute* 57(4): 176–82.

Arrow, K. R. (1967) 'Values and collective decision-making', in E. S. Phelps (ed.) *Economic Justice*, Harmondsworth: Penguin, 1973.

Atiyah, P. S. (1980) *Accidents, Compensation and the Law*, 3rd edn, London: Weidenfeld & Nicolson.

Bachrach, P. and Baratz, M. S. (1970) *Power and Poverty: Theory and Practice*, Oxford: Oxford University Press.

Bahr, H. (1973) *Skid Row*, New York: Oxford University Press.

Bailey, R. and Brake, M. (eds) (1975) *Radical Social Work*, London: Arnold.

Banting, K. G. (1979) *Poverty, Politics and Policy: Britain in the 1960s*, London: Macmillan.

Barnes, J. and Lucas, H. (1975) 'Positive discrimination in education', in J. Barnes (ed.), *Educational Priority*, vol. 3 London: HMSO.

Barry, B. (1965) *Political Argument*, London: Routledge & Kegan Paul.

(1973) *The Liberal Theory of Justice*, Oxford: Clarendon Press.

Becker, H. (1963) *Outsiders: Studies in the Sociology of Deviance*, New York: Free Press.

Beer, S. H. (1982) *Modern British politics*, 3rd edn, London: Faber & Faber.

Beerman, R. (1960) 'The law against parasites, tramps and beggars', *Soviet Studies* 11(4): 453–5.

Benn, S. I. and Peters, R. S. (1959) *Social Principles and the Democratic State*, London: Allen & Unwin.

Bentham, J. (1789) 'An introduction to the principles of morals and legislation', in M. Warnock (ed.) *Utilitarianism*, Glasgow: Collins, 1962.

Berger, P. and Luckmann, T. (1967) *The Social Construction of Reality*, New York: Anchor.

Berki, R. N. (1979) 'State and society: an antithesis of modern political thought', in J. Hayward and R. N. Berki, *State and Society in Contemporary Europe*, Oxford: Martin Robertson.

Berlin, I. (1969) *Four Essays on Liberty*, Oxford: Oxford University Press.

Bernstein, S. (1975) 'Self-determination: king or citizen in the realm of values?', in F. McDermott (ed.) *Self-determination in Social Work*, London: Routledge & Kegan Paul.

Beveridge, W. (1942) *Social Insurance and Allied Services* (Beveridge Report), Cmd 6404 London: HMSO.

Blacker, C. P. (ed.) (1952) *Problem Families: Five Inquiries*, London: Eugenics Society.

Blau, P. M. (1964) *Exchange and Power in Social Life*, New York: John Wiley.

Blaxter, M. (1974) 'Health "on the welfare" – a case study', *Journal of Social Policy* 3(1): 39–51.

Bottomore, T. (1966) *Elites and Society*, Harmondsworth: Penguin.

Boulding, K. (1973) 'The boundaries of social policy', in W. D. Birrell, P. A. R. Hillyard, A. S. Murie, and D. J. D. Roche (eds) *Social Administration: Readings in Applied Social Science*, Harmondsworth: Penguin.

Bowie, N. E. and Simon R. L. (1977) *The Individual and the Political Order*, Englewood Cliffs; NJ: Prentice-Hall.

Bradshaw, J. (1972) 'A taxonomy of social need', in G. MacLachlan (ed.) *Problems and Progress in Medical Care* (7th series), Oxford: Oxford University Press.

Bramsted, E. K. and Melhuish, K. J. (eds) (1978) *Western Liberalism*, London: Longman.

Brennan, G. and Friedman, D. (1981) 'A libertarian perspective on welfare', in P. G. Brown, C. Johnson, and P. Vernier (eds) *Income Support: Conceptual and Policy Issues*, Totowa, NJ: Rowman & Littlefield.

Briggs, A. (1961) 'The welfare state in historical perspective', *European Journal of Sociology* 2: 221–58.

Brown, J. C. (1984) *Disability Income, Part II: The Disability Income System*, London: Policy Studies Institute.

Brown, M. and Madge, N. (1982) *Despite the Welfare State*, London: Heinemann.

Buck, P. W. (ed.) (1975) *How Conservatives Think*, Harmondsworth: Penguin.

Burke, E. (1790) *Reflections on the Revolution in France*, New York: Holt, Rinehart, & Winston, 1959.

Byrne, A. and Padfield, C. F. (1978) *Social Services Made Simple*, London: W. H. Allen.

Byrne, D. (1987) 'Rich and poor: the growing divide', in A. Walker and C. Walker (eds) *The Growing Divide: a Social Audit 1979–1987*, London: Child Poverty Action Group.

Campbell, T. (1983) *The Left and Rights: A Conceptual Analysis of the Idea of Socialist Rights*, London: Routledge & Kegan Paul.

Cawson, A. (1982) *Corporatism and Welfare*, London: Heinemann.

Central Statistical Office (CSO) (1986) *Social Trends 16*, London: HMSO.

Charvet, J. (1983) 'The idea of equality as a substantive principle of society', in W. Letwin (ed.) *Against Equality*, London: Macmillan.

Checkland, S. G. and Checkland, O. (eds) (1974) *The Poor Law Report of 1834*, Harmondsworth: Penguin.

Clarke, D. (1975) 'The Conservative faith in a modern age', in P. W. Buck (ed.) *How Conservatives Think*, Harmondsworth: Penguin.

Clinard, M. B. (ed.) (1968) *Sociology of Deviant Behaviour*, 3rd edn, New York: Holt, Rinehart, & Winston.

Cmnd 7054 (1978) *Report of the Royal Commission on Civil Liability for Personal Injury*, London: HMSO.

Cmnd 9518 (1985) *Reform of Social Security*, vol. 2, London: HMSO.

Cohen, A. K. (1966) *Deviance and Control*, Englewood Cliffs, NJ: Prentice-Hall.

Constant, B. (1815) 'Principes de politique', in B. Constant, *Oeuvres*, Paris: Editions Gallimard, 1957.

Craddock, J. (1975) *Tenants Participation in Housing Management*, London: Association of London Housing Estates.

Cranston, M. (1976) 'Human rights, real and supposed', in N. Timms and D. Watson (eds) *Talking about Welfare*, London Routledge & Kegan Paul.

Crosland, C. A. R. (1956) *The Future of Socialism* London: Jonathan Cape.

Dahl, R. A. (1956) *A Preface to Democratic Theory*, Chicago: University of Chicago Press.

    (1961) *Who Governs?* New Haven Conn.: Yale University Press.

Damer, S. and Hague, C. (1971) 'Public participation in planning: a review', *Town Planning Review*, 42: 217–32.

DES (UK Department of Education and Science): Central Advisory Council on Education (England) (1967) *Children and Their Primary Schools*, vol. 1, London: HMSO.

DHSS (UK Department of Health and Social Security) (1974) *Report of the Committee of Inquiry into the Care and Supervision of Maria Colwell*, London: HMSO.

    (1980) *Inequalities in Health*, London: HMSO.

DoE (UK Department of the Environment) (1969) *People and Planning: Report of the Committee on Public Participation in Planning*, London: HMSO.

Dilnot, A. W., Kay, J. A., and Morris, C. N. (1984) *The Reform of Social Security*, Oxford: Institute of Fiscal Studies, Oxford University Press.

Drake, M., O'Brien, M., and Biebuyck, T. (1981) *Single and Homeless*, London: UK Department of the Environment.

Dworkin, G. (1979) 'Paternalism', in P. Laslett and J. Fishkin (eds) *Philosophy, Politics and Society*, 5th series, Oxford: Blackwell.

    (1981) 'Paternalism and welfare', in P. G. Brown *et al.* (eds) *Income Support: Conceptual and Policy Issues*, Totowa, NJ: Rowman & Littlefield.

Dworkin R. (1978) *Taking Rights Seriously*, London: Duckworth.

    (1985) *A Matter of Principle*, Cambridge, Mass.: Harvard University Press.

The Economist (1966) 'The distribution and taxation of wealth', in J. Urry and J. Wakefield (eds) *Power in Britain*, London: Heinemann, 1973.

Eccleshall, R., Geoghegan, V., Jay, R., and Wilford, R. (1984) *Political Ideologies: An Introduction*, London: Hutchinson.

The Federalist Papers (1787–8), New York: New American Library, 1961.

Feinberg, J. (1973) *Social philosophy*, Englewood Cliffs, NJ: Prentice Hall.
  (1980) *Rights, Justice and the Bounds of Liberty*, Princeton, NJ: Princeton University Press.
Ferge, Z. (1979) *A Society in the Making: Hungarian Social and Societal Policy 1945–1975*, Harmondsworth: Penguin.
Finch, J. (1984) *Education as Social Policy*, London: Longman.
Flew, A. (1981) *The Politics of Procrustes*, London: Temple Smith.
Forder, A. (1974) *Concepts in Social Administration*, London: Routledge & Kegan Paul.
Forder, A., Caslin, T., Pontin, G., and Walklate (1984) *Theories of Welfare*, London: Routledge & Kegan Paul.
Freeman, M. D. A. (1983) *The Rights and Wrongs of Children*, London: Frances Pinter.
Friedman, M. (1962) *Capitalism and Freedom*, Chicago: University of Chicago Press.
Friedman, M. and Friedman R. (1981) *Free to Choose*, Harmondsworth: Penguin.
Galbraith, J. K. (1972) *The New Industrial State*, rev. edn, Harmondsworth: Penguin.
George, V. and Manning, N. (1980) *Socialism, Social Welfare and the Soviet Union*, London: Routledge & Kegan Paul.
George, V. and Wilding, P. (1977) *Ideology and Social Welfare*, 2nd edn, London: Routledge & Kegan Paul, 1985.
Gerard, D. (1985) 'What makes a volunteer?', *New Society*, 8 Nov., pp. 236–8.
Giddens, A. (1976) *New Rules of Sociological Method*, London: Hutchinson.
Ginsburg, N. (1979) *Class, Capital and Social Policy*, London: Macmillan.
Goffman, E. (1963) *Stigma: Notes on the Management of Spoiled Identity*, Harmondsworth: Penguin, 1968.
Goodin, R. E. (1982) *Political Theory and Public Policy*, Chicago: University of Chicago Press.
Gould, B. and Topliss, E. (1981) *A Charter for the Disabled*, Oxford: Blackwell.
Greve, J. (1975) 'Comparisons, perspectives', in E. Butterworth and R. Holman (eds) *Social Welfare in Modern Britain*, Glasgow: Collins.
Habermas, J. (1976) *Legitimation Crisis*, London: Heinemann.
  (1984) 'What does a legitimation crisis mean today? Legitimation problems in late capitalism', in W. Connolly (ed.) *Legitimacy and the State*, Oxford: Blackwell.
Halifax (1684) 'The character of a trimmer', in J. P. Kenyon (ed.) *Halifax: Complete Works*, Harmondsworth: Penguin, 1969.
Hall, P. (1975) *Urban and Regional Planning*, Newton Abbot: David & Charles.
Ham, C. and Hill, M. (1984) *The Policy Process in the Modern Capitalist State*, Brighton: Wheatsheaf.
Harris, A. (1971) *Handicapped and Impaired in Britain*, vol. 1, London: HMSO.
Harris, J. (1982) 'The political status of children', in K. Graham (ed.) *Contemporary Political Philosophy*, Cambridge: Cambridge University Press.

Hart, H. L. A. (1955) 'Are there any natural rights?', *Philosophical Review* 64: 175–91.

Hartley, L. P. (1960) *Facial Justice*, London: Hamish Hamilton.

Harvey, D. (1973) *Social Justice and the City*, London: Arnold.

Hayek, F. (1944) *The Road to Serfdom*, London: Routledge & Kegan Paul.

(1976) *Law, Legislation and Liberty Vol. 2: The Mirage of Social Justice*, London: Routledge & Kegan Paul.

(1984) 'Equality, value and merit', in M. Sandel (ed.) *Liberalism and Its Critics*, Oxford: Blackwell.

Heller, A. (1976) *The Theory of Need in Marx*, London: Allison & Busby.

Higgins, J. (1980) 'Social control theories of social policy', *Journal of Social Policy* 9(1): 1–23.

Hobbes, T. (1651) *Leviathan*, ed. C. B. MacPherson, Harmondsworth: Penguin, 1968.

Homans, G. C. (1961) *Social Behaviour: Its Elementary Forms*, London: Routledge & Kegan Paul.

ICSW: International Council on Social Welfare (1969) *Social Welfare and Human Rights*, New York: Columbia University Press.

ILO: International Labour Office (1984) *Into the twenty-first century: the development of social security*, Geneva: ILO.

Janowitz, M. (1976) *Social Control of the Welfare State*, New York: Elsevier.

Jones, C. (1983) *State Social Work and the Working Class*, London: Macmillan.

(1985) *Patterns of Social Policy*, London: Tavistock.

Jones, K., Brown, J., and Bradshaw, J. (1978) *Issues in Social Policy*, London: Routledge & Kegan Paul.

Jordan, B. (1973) *Paupers*, London: Routledge & Kegan Paul.

(1987a) 'The moral basis of social provision', unpublished paper.

(1987b) *Rethinking Welfare*, Oxford: Blackwell.

Joseph, K. and Sumption, J. (1979) *Equality*, London: John Murray.

Judge, K. and Knapp, M. (1985) 'Efficiency in the production of welfare: the public and private sectors compared', in R. Klein and M. O'Higgins (eds) *The Future of Welfare*, Oxford: Blackwell.

Keller, S. (1963) *Beyond the Ruling Class*, New York: Random House.

Keynes, J. M. (1936) *The General Theory of Employment, Interest and Money*, London: Macmillan.

Lee, J. M. (1963) *Social Leaders and Public Persons*, Oxford; Oxford University Press.

Le Grand, J. (1982) *The Strategy of Equality*, London: Allen & Unwin.

(1984) 'The future of the welfare state', *New Society*, 7 June, pp. 385–6.

Le Grand, J. and Robinson, R. (1976) *The Economics of Social Problems*, London: Macmillan.

Lemert, E. M. (1951) *Social Pathology*, New York: McGraw-Hill.

Lenin, V. I. (1918, 2nd edn) *The State and Revolution*, London: Central Books, 1972.

Lévi-Strauss, C. (1949) *The Elementary Structures of Kinship*, trans J. H. Bell,

J. R. von Sturmer, and R. Needham, rev. edn, London: Eyre & Spottiswoode, 1969.

Little, I. M. D. (1957) *A Critique of Welfare Economics*, 2nd edn, Oxford: Oxford University Press.

Lively, J. (1975) *Democracy*, Oxford: Blackwell.

Locke, J. (1690) *Two Treatises of Civil Government*, ed. P. Laslett, New York: Mentor, 1965.

Lucas, J. R. (1966) *The Principles of Politics*, Oxford: Clarendon Press.

Lukes, S. (1978) 'Power and authority', in T. Bottomore and R. Nisbet (eds) *A History of Sociological Analysis*, London: Heinemann.

Lyall, J. (1980) 'Why the furry, feathery and four-footed pull in the cash', *Guardian*, 29 Dec., p. 8.

Lynes, T. (1969) *Welfare Rights*, London: Fabian Society.

McAuley, A. N. D. (1977) *Soviet Anti-poverty Policy 1955–1975*, University of Essex Department of Economics, Colchester.

MacCallum, G. (1967) 'Negative and positive freedom', *Philosophical Review* 76: 312–34.

Macey, J. P. (1982) *Housing Management*, 4th edn, London: Estate Gazette.

Mack, J. and Lansley, S. (1985) *Poor Britain*, London: Allen & Unwin.

Mannheim, K. (1936) *Ideology and Utopia*, trans. I. Wirth and E. Shils, London: Routledge & Kegan Paul.

Marshall, T. H. (1963) *Sociology at the Crossroads*, London: Heinemann.
(1981) *The Right to Welfare*, London: Heinemann.

Marx, K. (1844) 'Economic and philosophical manuscripts', in D. McLellan (ed.) *Karl Marx: Selected Writings*, Oxford: Oxford University Press, 1977.
(1875) 'Critique of the Gotha Programme', in K. Marx and F. Engels, *Selected Works*, London: Lawrence & Wishart, 1968.

Marx, K. and Engels, F. (1848) *The Communist Manifesto*, Harmondsworth: Penguin, 1967.

Maslow, A. H. (1943) 'A theory of human motivation', *Psychological Review* 50: 370–96.

Mauss, M. (1925) *The Gift: Forms and Functions of Exchange in Archaic Societies*, trans. I. Cunnison, London: Cohen & West, 1966.

Merton, R. K. (1968) *Social Theory and Social Structure*, New York: Free Press, 1968.

Miliband, R. (1969) *The State in Capitalist Society*, London: Weidenfeld & Nicolson.

Mill, J. S. (1859) 'On Liberty', in M. Warnock (ed.) *Utilitarianism*, Glasgow: Collins, 1962.

Miller, D. (1976) *Social Justice*, Oxford: Oxford University Press.

Mishra, R. (1981) *Society and Social Policy*, 2nd edn, London: Macmillan.

Mooney, G. H., Russell, E. M., and Weir, R. D. (1980) *Choices for Health Care*, London: Macmillan.

New Society (1969) 'Pensions progress', 30 Jan. p. 155.

Nirje, B. (1972) 'The right to self-determination', in W. Wolfensberger (ed.),

The Principle of Normalisation in Human Services, Toronto: National Institute on Mental Retardation.

Nozick, R. (1974) *Anarchy, State and Utopia,* Oxford: Blackwell.

Oakeshott, M. (1975) 'The vocabulary of a modern European state', *Political Studies* 23(2–3): 319–41.

O'Connor, J. (1973) *The Fiscal Crisis of the State,* New York: St Martin's Press.

Offe, C. (1984) *Contradictions of the Welfare State,* London: Hutchinson.

O'Higgins, M. (1985) 'Welfare, redistribution and inequality – disillusion, illusion and reality', in Bean, P., Ferris, J., and Whynes, D. (eds) *In Defence of Welfare,* London: Tavistock.

—— (1987) 'Egalitarians, equalities and welfare evaluation', *Journal of Social Policy* 16(1): 1–18.

Olson, M. (1971) *The Logic of Collective Action: Public Goods and the Theory of Groups,* rev. edn, Cambridge, Mass.: Harvard University Press.

Open University (1985) *Social Policy and Social Welfare,* Milton Keynes: Open University Press.

Orbach, L. F. (1977) *Homes for Heroes,* London: Seeley Service.

Pahl, J. (1985) 'Who benefits from Child Benefit?', *New Society,* 25 April, pp. 117–19.

Pen, J. (1974) *Income Distribution,* Harmondsworth: Penguin.

Perlman, H. H. (1975) 'Self-determination: reality or illusion?', in F. McDermott (ed.) *Self-determination in Social Work,* London: Routledge & Kegan Paul.

Phillips, D. L. (1963) 'Rejection: a possible consequence of seeking help for mental disorders', *American Sociological Review* 28(6): 963–72.

—— (1966) 'Public identification and acceptance of the mentally ill', *American Journal of Public Health and the Nation's Health* 56(5): 755–63.

Phillips, M. H. (1981) 'Favourable family impact as an objective of means support policy', in P. G. Brown *et al.* (eds) *Income Support: Conceptual and Policy Issues,* Totowa, NJ: Rowman & Littlefield.

Pinker, R. A. (1971) *Social Theory and Social Policy,* London: Heinemann.

Piven, F. and Cloward, R. (1972) *Regulating the Poor: The Functions of Public Welfare,* London: Tavistock.

Plant, R. (1984) 'The resurgence of ideology', in H. Drucker, P. Dunleavy, A. Gamble, and G. Peele (eds) *Developments in British Politics,* London: Macmillan.

Plant, R., Lesser, H., and Taylor-Gooby, P. (1980) *Political Philosophy and Social Welfare,* London: Routledge & Kegan Paul.

Polanyi, G., and Wood, J. B. (1974) 'How unevenly is wealth spread today?', in W. Letwin (ed.) *Against Equality,* London: Macmillan, 1983.

Popper, K. (1945) *The Open Society and Its Enemies, Vol. 2,* London: Routledge.

Poulantzas, N. (1978) *State, Power, Socialism,* trans. P. Camiller, London: NLB.

Power, A. (1981) 'How to rescue council housing', *New Society,* 4 June: 388–9.

PSI: Policy Studies Institute (1984) *The reform of Supplementary Benefit: working papers*, London: PSI.

Rae, D. (1981) *Equalities*, Cambridge, Mass.: Harvard University Press.

Raphael, D. D. (1976) *Problems of Political Philosophy*, London: Macmillan.

Rawls, J. (1971) *A Theory of Justice*, Oxford: Oxford University Press.

(1982) 'Social unity and primary goods', in A. Sen and B. Williams (eds) *Utilitarianism and Beyond*, Cambridge: Cambridge University Press.

Reddin, M. (1970) 'Universality versus selectivity', in W. A. Robson and B. Crick (eds) *The future of the social services*, Harmondsworth: Penguin.

Rein, M. (1983) *From policy to practice*, London: Macmillan.

Rein, M. and van Gunsteren, H. (1984) 'The dialectic of public and private pensions', *Journal of Social Policy* 14(2): 129–50.

Richardson, A. (1983) *Participation*, London: Routledge and Kegan Paul.

Robson, W. A. (1976) *Welfare State and Welfare Society*, London: Allen & Unwin.

Room, G. (1979) *The Sociology of Welfare*, Oxford: Martin Robertson.

Rousseau, J. J. (1762) 'The social contract', in E. Barker (ed.) *Social Contract*, Oxford: Oxford University Press, 1971.

Russell, B. (1960) *Power*, London: Unwin.

Sahlins, M. (1974) *Stone Age Economics*, London: Tavistock.

Saunders, P. (1979) *Urban Politics*, Harmondsworth: Penguin.

Schaar, J. H. (1971) 'Equality of opportunity, and beyond', in A. de Crespigny and A. Wertheimer (eds) *Contemporary Political Theory*, London: Nelson.

Schoek, H. (1969) *Envy*, trans. G. M. Glenny and B. Ross, New York: Harcourt Brace, World.

Schumpeter, J. (1967) 'Two concepts of democracy', in A. Quinton (ed.), *Political Philosophy*, Oxford: Oxford University Press.

Scott, R. A. (1969) *The Making of Blind Men*, New York: Russell Sage Foundation.

Segal, S. P. (1978) 'Attitudes towards the mentally ill: a review', *Social Work* 23(3): 211–17.

Seldon, A. (1977) *Charge!* London: Temple Smith.

Silver, H. (ed.) (1973) *Equal Opportunity in Education*, London: Methuen.

Simmel, G. (1908) 'The Poor', trans. C. Jacobson, *Social Problems* 13 (Fall 1965): 118–39.

(1950) *The Sociology of Georg Simmel*, ed. and trans. K. Wolff, New York: Free Press.

Soyer, D. (1975) 'The right to fail', in F. McDermott (ed.) *Self-determination in Social Work*, London: Routledge & Kegan Paul.

Spencer, J. C. (1963) 'The multi-problem family', in B. Schlesinger (ed.) *The Multi-Problem Family*, Toronto: University of Toronto Press.

Spicker, P. (1984) *Stigma and Social Welfare*, Beckenham: Croom Helm.

(1985) 'Why freedom implies equality', *Journal of Applied Philosophy* 2(2): 205–16.

Steenbergen, B. van (1983) 'The sociologist as social architect: a new task for macro-sociology?', *Futures* 15(5): 376–81.

Steiner, H. (1981) 'Liberty and equality', *Political Studies* 29(4): 555–69.

Sugden, R. (1980) 'Altruism, duty and the welfare state', in N. Timms (ed.) *Social Welfare: Why and How?* London: Routledge & Kegan Paul.

Szamuely, T. (1971) 'Russia and Britain: comprehensive inequality', in C. Cox and A. E. Dyson, *The Black Papers in Education*, London: Davis-Poynter.

Tawney, R. H. (1926) *Religion and the Rise of Capitalism*, Harmondsworth: Penguin, 1938.

(1931) *Equality*, London: Unwin, 1964.

Taylor, C. (1979) 'What's wrong with negative liberty?' in A. Ryan (ed.) *The Idea of Freedom*, Oxford: Oxford University Press.

Taylor-Gooby, P. and Dale, J. (1981) *Social theory and social welfare*, London: Arnold.

Theones, P. (1966) *The Élite in the Welfare State*, London: Faber.

Thomson, J. A. K. (1953) *The Ethics of Aristotle*, Harmondsworth: Penguin.

Titmuss, R. M. (1955a) 'The social division of welfare: some reflections on the search for equity' in *Essays on 'the Welfare State'*, 2nd edn, London: Allen & Unwin, 1963.

(1955b) 'War and social policy', in *Essays on 'the Welfare State'*, 2nd edn, London: Allen & Unwin, 1963.

(1968) *Commitment to Welfare*, London: Allen & Unwin.

(1970) *The Gift Relationship*, Harmondsworth: Penguin.

(1974) *Social Policy: An Introduction*, London: Allen & Unwin.

Townsend, P. (1976) *Sociology and Social Policy*, Harmondsworth: Penguin.

(1979) *Poverty in the United Kingdom*, Harmondsworth: Penguin.

Trattner, W. (1974) *From Poor Law to Welfare State: A History of Social Welfare in America*, New York: Free Press.

Turner, J. F. C. (1969) 'Uncontrolled urban settlement: problems and policies', in G. Breese (ed.) *The City in Newly Developing Countries*, Englewood Cliffs, NJ: Prentice-Hall.

Uttley, S. (1980) 'The welfare exchange reconsidered', *Journal of Social Policy* 9(2): 187–205.

Veit Wilson, J. (1983) 'Seebohm Rowntree and the poor', *New Society*, 20 Jan: 97–9.

Walzer, M. (1984) 'Welfare, membership and need', in M. Sandel (ed.) *Liberalism and Its Critics*, Oxford: Blackwell.

Ward, C. (1974) *Tenants Take Over*, London: Architectural Press.

Watson, D. (1977) 'Welfare rights and human rights', *Journal of Social Policy* 6(1): 31–46.

Weale, A. (1978) 'Paternalism and social policy', *Journal of Social Policy* 7(2): 157–72.

(1983) *Political Theory and Social Policy*, London: Macmillan.

Weber, M. (1967) 'The development of caste', in R. Bendix and S. M. Lipset, *Class, Status and Power*, 2nd edn, London: Routledge & Kegan Paul.

Wedge, P. and Prosser, H. (1973) *Born to Fail?* London: Arrow.

Weisbrod, B. A. (1970) *On the Stigma Effect and the Demand for Welfare Programs*, Madison, Wisc.: Institute for Research on Poverty.

Wilding, P. and George, V. (1975) 'Social value and social policy', *Journal of Social Policy* 4(4): 373–90.

Wilson, D. (1979) *The Welfare State in Sweden*, London: Heinemann.

Wolfenden Committee (1977) *The Future of Voluntary Organizations*, Beckenham: Croom Helm.

Wright, D. (1971) *The Psychology of Moral Behaviour*, Harmondsworth: Penguin.

Wright Mills, C. (1956) *The Power Élite*, New York: Oxford University Press.

Name index

Ackerman, B. 66
Alchian, A. A. 34
Allen, W. R. 34
Amdur, R. 140–1
Aristotle, 136
Arnstein, S. R. 97, 102
Arrow, K. R. 14
Atiyah, P. S. 141

Bachrach, P. 102, 148
Bahr, H. 42
Bailey, R. 52
Banting, K. G. 92–3
Baratz, M. S. 102, 148
Barnes, J. 131
Barry, B. 9, 10, 135, 153
Becker, H. 28
Beer, S. H. 167–8
Beerman, R. 17
Benn, S. I. 58, 80, 91, 128
Bentham, J. 10, 12
Berger, P. 21
Berki, R. N. 81
Berlin, I. 44, 45
Bernstein, S. 50
Beveridge, W. 24, 76, 164
Biebuyck, T. 42
Blacker, C. P. 28
Blau, P. M. 37
Blaxter, M. 70
Booth, C. 6
Bottomore, T. 100
Boulding, K. 18, 13, 101
Bowie, N. E. 12, 133
Bradshaw, J. 5, 8, 32–3
Brake, M. 52
Brennan, G. 82, 138–9

Briggs, A. 76
Brown, J. 5, 32–3
Brown, J. C. 141, 143
Brown, M. 126, 148
Burke, E. 21, 42, 82, 153, 168, 169
Byrne, D. 113

Campbell, T. 63, 69–70
Cawson, A. 85
Central Statistical Office (CSO)
    112, 113, 119
Charvet, J. 127
Checkland, S. 27
Clarke, D. 168–9
Cloward, R. 102
Cohen, A. K. 27
Constant, B. 94
Craddock, J. 97
Cranston, M. 61, 62
Crosland, C. A. R. 108, 118, 129,
    130, 149, 154, 163, 164, 165–7,
    169

Dahl, R. A. 9, 100–1
Dale, J. vii, 165
Damer, S. 95
Darwin, C. 168
DES (UK Department of
    Education and Science) 131–2
DHSS (UK Department of Health
    and Social Security) 110
Dilnot, A. W. 153
Disraeli, B. 168
DoE (UK Department of the
    Environment) 96
Drake, M. 42, 43
Dworkin, G. 54, 55

184   PRINCIPLES OF SOCIAL WELFARE

Subject index